MUD MAP TO AUKUS

The Crucible of a Pacific War

Philip Du Rhone

for N.K. Meaney

Published by Hybrid Publishers

Melbourne Victoria Australia

© Philip du Rhone 2021

www.hybridpublishers.com.au

First published 2022

A catalogue record for this book is available from the National Library of Australia

ISBN 978-1-925736-98-4 (p)

ISBN 978-1-925736-97-7 (e)

Cover design, typesetting and layout: Bruce Welch

CONTENTS

ACKNOWLEDGEMENTS

My thanks are due to several people in particular, spread over the more-than-50 years of this book's making.

Firstly, I am grateful to Dr. N.K. (Neville) Meaney of Sydney University who first inspired then guided me in the work that was carried out, providing regular encouragement and suggestions without insisting on undue restrictions.

I am indebted also to Vivien Price, B.Sc. of Sydney University who gave a great deal of time and practical help which included proofing and typing the first draft from my hand-written original, suggesting edits and carrying out all the photographic work. Without her generous involvement the images in the Appendix at least would certainly not have appeared in the thesis.

More recently my gratitude to Bruce Welch who spun his digital magic over a dusty, old, typed manuscript and brought it to new life, revitalising the images along the way through his patience and tenacity with internet searching (and to Trove for making those images available); to Nola Pearce at Balmain Library for her time and effort in transferring the manuscript to digital form; and to Chaia, Christel, Anya and Carol for their usual invaluable advice.

Mud Map to AUKUS

PREAMBLE

THIS book is the by-product of a study carried out in 1969 and written for the purpose of a History Honours degree at the University of Sydney. It is being published now as it may afford some valuable addition to the scholarly and public process of understanding the nature of the latest Indo-Pacific security arrangement Australia has entered into with the United Kingdom and the United States, known as AUKUS, and how it came to be. The study has been re-worked but only slightly, since the key element – the information available from that time – has not changed, nor my interpretation of it. Some currency has been occasionally injected in small measure to place the topic into contemporary context. Essential or revealing footnotes have been incorporated into the text but most have been deleted for the purpose of readability. Full textual references and attributions may be found in the original work held by the History Department at the University of Sydney.

PREFACE

THE recent military security agreement between the Governments of Australia, the United Kingdom and the United States has brought the nature of Australia's overall national defence arrangements under renewed scrutiny. Yet the roots of AUKUS go back many decades, indeed centuries. Its nature is determined by this historical background and dictated by the geopolitical reality. There is much to be grateful for being at the "arse end" of the world, geographically, in Paul Keating's words.

In 1908 Prime Minister Alfred Deakin invited – personally to President Roosevelt – the US Great White Fleet to visit Australia. Her Majesty's Government was not amused by this precociousness and it was very much to the chagrin of the British Admiralty. Deakin in many ways pre-empted by 33 years wartime Prime Minister John Curtin's historic call to America, though the latter's was far more crucial. Most of the population of Sydney turned out around the harbour in party mood to see the American ships, Melbourne followed soon after in much the same spirit, an expression of public opinion as powerful as any, perhaps. It was as much the draw of a spectacle as anything. The Americans were an appealing curiosity. A British fleet would have been like a boring family get-together.

Mud Map to AUKUS

In 1911 Australian Navy ships were granted the title HMAS, His Majesty's Australian rather than just His Majesty's Ships, but His Majesty's nevertheless. They remain to this day His, or Hers. The Australian navy remained at the disposal of the British and was placed under their complete authority at the outbreak of WW1. Australia's first submarines, the uninspiringly named AE1 and AE2, were commissioned in 1914 and were both lost under Royal Navy command. More poor-quality submarines followed in the inter-war years, none of them worthy of active service, and either were returned to the seller or scuttled. The only submarine operated by Australia during WW2, acquired just before the 1943 election, was yet another cast-off, this time from the Dutch, and was so inadequate it was used solely for training purposes and lasted less than one year. This history did not auger well for any future submarine project in Australia. On the other hand, Brisbane and Fremantle became critical as bases for the execution of the war in the Pacific, again giving some indication of how Australia may best serve the interests of any security strategy for the Indo-Pacific.

That message from John Curtin to the Australian people about Australia's newly perceived and immediate security needs was published in the *Melbourne Herald* on December 27, 1941, three

12

weeks after the Japanese attack on Pearl Harbor, and when Japan's intentions were obvious and menacing. "Without any inhibitions of any kind, I make it quite clear that Australia looks to America, free of any pangs as to our traditional links or kinship with the United Kingdom." This came not long after another Australian Prime Minister, R.G. Menzies, had expressed in a broadcast speech the melancholy logic of Australia being at war as a consequence of Great Britain being at war. In both cases the invocation was formulated in terms of race and a culture, what today might be euphemistically, or adventurously, described as the "anglosphere".

President Roosevelt's speech following Japan's "dastardly" attack is famous for its description of that "day of infamy", but it finished with a promise more relevant to today's security planning, that America would "make certain that this form of treachery shall never endanger us again". That was a promise that Australia could safely live with.

Two months earlier, in October, 1941, a Labor Government had begun its eight years in office, taking over from an ironically named disunited and discredited United Australia Party–United Country Party coalition led by Menzies who had spent three months leading from overseas the nation

Mud Map to AUKUS

at war. It was the only period of a protracted Labor Government up to then, and until surpassed by the Hawke Labor Government 40 years later. Hence, it was a period which afforded Labor the opportunity of implementing more than just piecemeal policy – of actually infusing into Australian foreign policy a general element of fundamentally Labor political philosophy. Additionally, for the first time, it allowed the Labor Party the luxury of developing its policies on the broader basis of its experience as a Government.

The importance of the above is emphasised by the fact that concurrently with the rule of the Labor Government in Australia there began the establishment of a new international organisation based on principles of justice, peace, freedom and equality. For the latent idealistic section of the Party this meant that Australian foreign policy could project itself into a universal concept of firmly based human welfare. For the more realistic it meant both hopes and problems. Sections of the powerful Australian labour movement also had half-buried, somewhat confused notions of a better world order – a product of its vague socialist heritage – and demanded that the opportunity not be wasted.

However, although this belief in international co-operation weighed heavily on Labor thinking. it was never allowed to cloud the issues. In so far as Labor developed an "independent" foreign policy it was "independent" in the sense that Labor was prepared to consider external affairs without automatic deference to another power's wishes. This does not mean Labor was prepared to act alone on matters of a serious nature, or undertake different preparations without taking into account the need for powerful support.

In the final analysis Labor did not gamble with Australian security by placing its entire confidence in the effectiveness of the United Nations as a peace-keeping organisation. Despite opposition (that is, the Liberal Country Party Opposition) claims to the contrary, the Labor Government kept power politics well in mind. In fact, as the decade drew to a close and the hopes diminished and the problems increased, Labor recognised more and more Australia's defence dependence.

The newly-found independent line which distinguished the post-war Labor Government's foreign policy had its roots in wartime diplomacy itself. It is interesting to speculate how far Australia's position as a smaller power during the war and its related attempts to secure a voice in wartime decisions led on to Evatt's insistence on the rights of smaller powers in the United Nations and in the Japanese Peace Treaty negotiations.

Post-war planning began in fact around 1940-41, as Paul Hasluck has pointed out, but actual formulation of ideas with a view to future action as opposed to immediate psychological and political propaganda requirements did not take place until 1943. It should be kept in mind then that thoughts on the post-war settlement took shape while hostilities were still being waged and while there was an intense desire for a peace which would be enduring and for an Australia which would be totally secure from the threat of attack. An effective United Nations coupled with a powerful defence arrangement satisfied this desire.

The earliest major concern of the Government was the position of Australia in the Pacific area. This, of course, was not an original concept, but there was a shift of emphasis when Curtin put forward his policy in 1941 and when it found form in the Australia-New Zealand Agreement in 1944. Australia was now to be the principal power in what can be described as the South-west Pacific and had a vital intertest in the islands to the north. But in future it was to act as the representative of the British Commonwealth – it was to be the "trustee of British civilisation" – not merely a participant but a leader in what Evatt called the "extended Australian zone". This was at once both a warning that Australia was not about to stand by and see what it regarded as its interests encroached upon, as well as the beginnings of a policy of regional security for the South-east Asian area.

Mud Map to AUKUS

The idea of regional security found favour amongst members of both political groups. Evatt early on saw regional security as an integral part of the framework of universal security, and later as a basic principle of United Nations security arrangements as incorporated in its Charter. Menzies and Spender agreed that Australia's main security interests lay in the islands to the north and north-west, Spender even talking of Australia's "vital and overriding" interests in New Caledonia and Portuguese Timor. But for them it was the emphasis on power that mattered – Australia's own power and the power of the British Empire and of the United States. Labor was finally forced to postpone any development of the regional security concept (though some foundations were laid for future successful attempts) because of the instability and confusion which were upsetting the power structure in Asia.

In relation to the regional security arrangement concept the United States gradually assumed a more and more important position in Australian defence thinking, partly because of the inadequacy of other regional arrangements, partly as an outcome of the development of the Japanese peace negotiations and partly as a response to the final acceptance of Britain's over-extended defence commitments. Nevertheless, the Government's attitude towards

Asian nations remained openly sympathetic. It recognised the growing and immediate need for Australia to establish a favourable impression with Asian countries and at the same time it recognised the reality of the progress of nationalist movements and the futility of attempting to arrest this progress – as Chifley said, it was like "poking a stick through water".

On this subject the differences that marked the policies of the Government and the Opposition can be seen clearly in their specific reactions to the Dutch-Indonesian crisis. While the Labor Government supported the Indonesians and combined with India to take the issue to the Security Council in July, 1947, and actually condemned the Netherlands in the Security Council in December, 1948, the Liberal Country Parties preferred to back the Dutch as more stable and trustworthy allies. The matter in fact provided the cause for the most heated debate over foreign policy during the period.

Another instance of this desire to come to grips with the realities of the new Asia was the caution displayed by all parties towards events in China. There was practically no sympathy in Australia for the Kuomintang, though, at the same time, there was a growing antipathy to anything labelled communist. Yet, by 1948, when the signs of the true nature of things in China became discernible, the Labor Government (and in fact the Liberal Country Opposition) was preparing to accept the inevitable state of affairs and recognise a Communist China.

The caution that was exhibited and the suppression of public airing of policies were primarily due to domestic considerations. The Labor Government's belief in regional harmony either within or outside the framework of the United Nations Charter extended to a tolerance of the existence of a Communist Government in the region.

In fact, this general tolerance accounted in some measure for the changing attitude assumed towards the Japanese Peace Treaty negotiations. It was at first an accepted fact to Australians that the Peace Treaty would contain the harshest possible terms for the Japanese. Yet by the time the Labor Party had lost office it was obvious that the Japanese had an essential place in American strategic considerations and that the Peace Treaty would be a very liberal one. This was conceded by Australia, again, not only because of the recognition of the need for American defence support, nor just because of the growing communist threat in east Asia, but also because Australia desired a free collaboration of healthy and friendly states to maintain the stability and development of the region.

Still, the simplicity of foreign policy which existed in the earlier half of the period was quickly giving way to a reaction to the huge power blocs that had developed. Despite opposition to the contrary again, Labor was not prepared in reality to give up "the substance for the shadow" (as Menzies put it). The United Nations became much as a by-play for the more concrete arrangements of co-operation with the Commonwealth and with the US for defence. The United States at first fitted into Labor's ideas as a vital part of its general Pacific or regional plan. Gradually, however, it assumed the role of the central de facto protector of Australia's security, requiring some reasonably guaranteed assurance the cost of which had yet to be reckoned. The Labor Government was willing to work and fight for the effectiveness of the United Nations as a peace-keeping force, but only on the basis that the world showed an equal willingness to accede to the principles on which it had been based and for which it was supposed to stand.

Though it was clear to all that Britain's future power in the "Far East" was uncertain, there was no lessening of the importance which both parties placed on Empire co-operation. Curtin, as early as 1943, was originating debate on the setting up of new post-war machinery for consultation and co-operation, including a permanent secretariat. There was no diminishing of the confidence displayed in the future functioning of combined Commonwealth forces in the defence of Pacific areas. There was a proud regard for the united and victorious front which the Empire had presented in the war, and for the example it exhibited to the world of an international organisation operating on a basis of freedom, equality and justice, however warped the understanding of the true situation was.

But this was in reality as far as it went for Labor. (It went a little further for the Opposition.) It needed no more than the experience of the war, in particular in the Pacific theatre, to indicate where Australia's future protection would come from. In the meantime, however, until public opinion had been carefully attuned to the new state of affairs, old relationships would not be hastily discarded.

There is also the matter of Labor's, or in reality Evatt's, part in the early work of the United Nations. It is true that a great deal of Evatt's energy and attention was applied to the idea of an international organisation and that the ALP strongly supported this strategy on the domestic front. A lot of what he said, however, was repetitious, and in many ways was aimed at building a favourable climate of public opinion. Most of the work, too, was concentrated on efforts to establish the United Nations on a firm basis, both technical and juridical, and then see that it functioned on such a basis. Australia's actions in the United Nations on such issues as Palestine, Indonesia, Greece and regional security were attempts to carry out the belief in orderly international affairs in practical terms, but were subsidiary to the mainstream of Australian foreign and defence policy.

Post-war policies included elements of a new independence plus elements of the old natural dependence. Evatt's stands were a continuation of his fight for more influence in the war effort, more importance for the Pacific war, and more weapons for Australia. Australia defied America and Britain in demanding representation at the armistice and peace arrangements. It combined with New Zealand in demanding a place in the Pacific settlement. It defied the Great Powers over the Security Council veto. It disagreed with the Soviets and annoyed and almost embarrassed the United States in Japan. It took the initiative over Indonesia. Yet it was clearly aware that in the event of a resurgent Japanese militarism, or a swift communist move southwards, it would be militarily helpless without Great Power support, and acted accordingly.

Evatt would undoubtedly have been very comfortable with the AUKUS arrangement.

FOREWORD

FEDERAL election campaigns are, by nature, widespread in their consequences and copious in their production of historical material. Although affected by wartime and post-war paper restrictions, the three campaigns, 1943, 1946, and 1949, which will be examined, are no exceptions. The intensity of their relatively brief lives is evidenced by the vast amount of information still available to the historian. Yet this extant material is small in comparison to the actual debate as it occurred in all its forms. A campaign is not limited to party leaders' statements, editorial policies, and official platforms. It includes all the minor candidates, successful or not, their supporting speakers, the door-to-door canvassers, and members of that nebulous group who either form an opinion or influence others to form one. The mass of participants in the debate are paid scant documentary attention indeed and their specific viewpoints are lost to posterity.

For these reasons the source materials on which this study is based are highly selective in two ways. Firstly there are the limitations imposed at the time by practical necessity – the scarcity of space in the larger newspapers, the impossibility of covering every aspect of the campaign or every meeting, the personal, geographical or ideological obscurity of most participants, the unrecorded nature of large sections of the debate – the reasons are various, but they act alike to doom much information to oblivion.

Secondly, there are the limitations imposed by the sheer profusion of sources, despite the selective process outlined above. There were, during the relevant period, over a dozen metropolitan daily newspapers operating, as well as innumerable smaller provincial, suburban and sectional presses. Most of the reporting was repetitious, but papers would obviously follow their own interests to the part exclusion of others'. Generally, the press religiously followed the four main personalities – John Curtin or J.B. (Ben) Chifley, H.V. (Herb) Evatt, R.G. (Robert) Menzies and A.W. (Arthur) Fadden – but they exercised their right to print whatever sections of a speech or statement they cared to. This situation is complicated by the fact that the party leaders carried on a national campaign, travelling extensively from one end of the continent to the other. The press could not always report on a personality consistently, and thus the cross-checking of newspapers becomes important for this reason alone.

One episode should illustrate the point sufficiently. J.P. Abbott, N.S.W. Country Party Member for New England, attacked Evatt over

Mud Map to AUKUS

Manus Island during a meeting in Scone, Tasmania. This was reported in the *Daily Telegraph (Sydney)* but not elsewhere. The next day, Evatt replied to Abbott at a meeting at Lindfield, Sydney, and though the *Sydney Morning Herald* reported the meeting his reply to Abbott is ignored. *The West Australian*, of Perth, carried this section of his speech. The next day in Brisbane, Chifley defended Evatt against Abbot's attack and it was reported in both *The Argus* (Melbourne) and the *Sydney Morning Herald*; the *Daily Telegraph* in Sydney carried the speech but excluded any mention of Evatt or of Manus Island. These were the only reports of the three-day incident in the newspapers examined.

Two major points stand out: newspapers did not necessarily follow up a story or print replies to criticism; and, a newspaper report did not necessarily depend on the proximity of the utterance. The upshot is that for a complete picture of the movement of a campaign, close attention must be paid to a selected number of reports and careful cross-checking must be undertaken to eliminate non-reporting and partial reporting in particular. Misreporting of election meetings in a few minor instances occurred, especially if the meetings were rowdy. Controversy did on one occasion continue for several days over what was said by an interjector and a speaker. the *Daily Telegraph* (Sydney) appears to be slightly suspect regarding such incidents.

The perennial problem of editorial bias is a constant danger especially during a period which was well suited to anti-Labor leanings. Almost all editorial policy was unfavourable to Labor, especially in 1946 and 1949, and too often this policy crept into the news sections. With sufficient care, however, a relatively balanced picture can be pieced together. *The West Australian* and *The Sydney Morning Herald* were usually fair in their reporting (with notable deviations), while *The Daily Telegraph* (Sydney) and *The Argus* (Melbourne) in 1946 were blatantly one-sided. (Brian Penton, editor of *The Daily Telegraph*, was fined by the Australian Journalists' Association for unethical practices.)

Nevertheless, the daily press remains the most important source of material for the election campaigns, and in many ways for the periods in between also. As P.D. Phillips put it:

… Ascertaining the broad outlines and expressed and underlying feelings of the people of a whole continent is a matter of peculiar difficulty … The difficulty of accurately estimating these popular feelings and trends in Australia is accentuated by the absence of the available masses of evidence so abundant in the United States and some other countries. Newspapers may not be infallible guides to opinion but other modes of investigation have been inadequately developed as yet …

Mud Map to AUKUS

The same may be as easily applied to the "public debate" as to "public opinion".

Other source material available related more to the public debate between the elections, and the movement and development of ideas in these periods. The Australian Public Opinion Poll began to conduct surveys during the period, and the results can be used as an interesting and helpful backdrop to the issues. They are, however, limited in their application because, briefly, they are very general and broad summaries of "public opinion" rather than articulate debate, and I have confined them to a consultative status.

Parliamentary Debates are similarly useful for expositions of policy and evidence of development, as well as for readily available material on the lesser reported campaign participants. However, once again, there are limitations especially in this period. The standard of the debates on foreign affairs was depressingly low once the party leaders had spoken. Interest in them was also short-lived, despite the fact that much criticism was levelled at the Government for the insufficient time allotted for such debate. One commentator described the scene during an important Ministerial statement from Evatt in February, 1947:

Most Labour members showed little interest in the foreign affairs speech, Mr. Ward was the only Minister who listened to Dr Evatt for the full 90 minutes. The Labour Member for Robertson, Mr. T.F. Williams, also sat it out, but appeared to be devoting most of his attention to answering correspondence. It cannot be said that the other side of the House gave the outline of world problems their undivided attention!

Such circumstances were not exceptional.

Mud Map to AUKUS

INTRODUCTION

THE extent to which the Australian electorate participates in the policy-making process of Government is limited by practical as well as political considerations. The transference of ideas and influence in politics is always a controversial issue: on the one hand, the force of public opinion acting upwards on political parties and leaders, and, on the other, the impress of party policy and politician's positions downwards on the people. In the case of foreign and defence policy the flow is more one-sided. Government often has a legitimate excuse – national security – for suppressing information, ignoring widespread opposition, or maintaining a strict silence where open debate would usually clarify national feeling. In fact, national attitudes to foreign and defence policy tend to follow Government policy rather than to change it, more so even than the nation itself realises. This study is concerned primarily with one aspect in the traffic of ideas on the subject of foreign and defence policy – the part taken by federal election campaigns, in particular, those of 1943, 1946, and 1949.

In considering the campaigns there will be a number of questions to be investigated. Firstly, however, it should be made clear that it is not the intention to discover "public opinion" or to come to a conclusion on the leanings of national feeling on various issues. The object of study is the national debate; the explanations, justifications, and arguments put forward for various cases supporting different viewpoints. Nor will Government policy as such (except in its relevance to the debate), be overly interpreted but the extent and manner in which it is publicly broadcast. The areas to which the post-war Labor Government applied itself in foreign affairs have been extensively covered by historians; the major interest here lies in how these issues were handled publicly during the brief periods given over to campaigning, and why they were so handled.

More specifically, questions to be kept in mind include whether election campaigns serve in any way to heighten or broaden discussion on particular aspects of foreign and defence policy, or whether the campaigns themselves act to modify or clarify the policies of the political parties or even those of individual participants If in fact the campaigns have any suchlike effect, can it be attributed to public reaction to the debate, strong Opposition criticism or a strong reactionary response to campaign factors such as the influence of domestic issues? Election campaigns have a place in the development of a nation's attitudes towards policy, therefore, it may be contended that political parties use the opportunity to test their policies with a view to discovering popular reaction to them. If this is in fact the case, then election campaigns hold an important place in any investigation of the development of national policies. Is it true? All these questions can be asked of any branch of policy debated in a campaign, therefore it is equally important to discover whether foreign and defence policy is treated any differently from other policies, how far they are interconnected, and what place they hold in the substantive policies of the parties.

More related to the topic are the actual issues raised in the debate. Were they merely side issues based on emphasis and methods rather than on matter? Was there general consensus among the parties on fundamental principles leading to a dampening effect on discussion? Or does any lack of discussion stem from the politicians' belief that the majority of the electorate are apathetic towards international affairs?

These are some of the general problems which will come into view as the campaigns unfold, but firstly it is useful to make a few comments on the nature of election campaigns and the place which foreign and defence policy has in them.

Four to five weeks is a very brief period in

which to debate and resolve successfully the whole gamut of national policy. This is the first factor which acts to limit the value of electioneering.

Secondly, the foremost aim of election campaigning is to secure more votes so that, more than at any other time, during election campaigns a political party must diffuse an air of calm confidence in its own policies, and must portray the opposing viewpoints as being unqualifiedly irresponsible and dangerous. Unity must be maintained and even slight disagreement avoided. The split between Menzies and Fadden in 1943 over post-war taxation credits, for instance, was catastrophic for the Opposition. Hence, points put forward tend to be in very simplistic, black and white terms, often generalised and usually platitudinous.

Thirdly, the participants in the campaign are not always the masters of the situation that they would like to be. A campaign can easily assume a wayward direction of its own. A slip of the tongue can be picked up by critics, magnified and turned into an issue. Debates can become bogged down in technical and useless arguments over side issues, to the partial exclusion of other issues and a general confounding of the whole campaign. Such was the case in 1943 when both Government and Opposition became involved in the controversy over who had "saved" Australia in 1942 and which resulted in a fruitless waste of time and energy.

Lastly, it is an accepted truism that electioneering is directed towards the populace in general, and towards the "swinging" vote in particular. For this reason policy must be clearcut and well-defined so that it may be readily grasped by the mass of voters. Rational, detailed and perceptive arguments as such do not necessarily register on the minds of voters who are only too anxious to reach a decision by reference to a simple and straightforward point. Should Australia seek to maintain the closest of relationships with Great Britain? Of course – few denied it either in 1943, 1946 or 1949. But if the Opposition could show neatly how the Government was going about destroying the British relationship, then no amount of sound and articulate reasoning on the latter's part need necessarily refute it.

The last limitation of election campaigns applies particularly to foreign and defence policy where issues are not always reducible to the type of struggle which takes place on the hustings. The other points, made on campaigns in general, are also applicable to foreign and defence policy. Brevity is not an advantage for a subject which calls for much thoughtful consideration. Black and white tones are not the best in which to view complex concepts and situations. Haphazard discussion of issues which should be carefully related is not conducive to a successful overall picture of a national policy of overriding importance. In short, election campaigns, especially with respect to foreign and defence policy, have serious drawbacks.

It is an established fact that foreign affairs had, up until 1966, never played a decisive part in the outcome of Australian federal elections. Arthur Calwell, ALP leader from 1960 to 1967, has expressed this view in his 1963 book, "Labor's Role In Modern Society", and he has been often quoted in support of the contention. The change which came about in this state of affairs in 1966 due to Australia's involvement in the Vietnam war was so drastic that Time Magazine, reporting on the 1969 federal elections, could casually and confidently state that "domestic issues … normally take second place to foreign affairs in Australian elections".

The exception which D.W. Rawson mentions in his 1966 book, "Labor In Vain?" – that of Curtin's war policy – is just that: an exception. The prosecution of the war was a vital issue at the 1943 elections, but it does not fit into the category of foreign affairs in the usual sense. Defence policy is not so much the neglected child of election campaigns as is foreign affairs, and certainly military conscription is always a potentially explosive issue in Australian politics.

This lack of general interest in foreign affairs during campaigns is attributable to numerous factors. Apathy on the part of not only the general public, but many of their elected representatives is certainly one. Menzies put this view smoothly at a press interview in Adelaide during the 1949 campaign. "Foreign affairs", he said, "would never be electioneering stuff in Australia because it had not a broad public appeal".

As has already been touched on, foreign policy does not invite itself for ready discussion in the atmosphere of intense electioneering. Also relevant is the fact that wide divergence between the two main parties or blocs in basic principles was not existent at the time, and debate was confined to methods and emphasis, therefore removing any basis for significant attacks. As Greenwood and Harper put it in their 1957 book, *Australia In World Affairs, 1950-1955*, when speaking of the neglect of foreign policy in the 1949 campaign:

There are a variety of reasons, and one is the regrettable fact that very few people in this country happen to be interested in other than domestic affairs … another reason is that there is no basic divergence between the parties; and thirdly, that the Opposition parties did not think they could, with any degree of success, attack the kind of policy that the Government had been pursuing overseas …

The last point is more applicable to the 1946 campaign than the 1949 campaign. In the latter, the Opposition were able to land some telling criticism of Evatt's handling of the portfolio as well as the apparent (or attempted) relaxing of the close relationships with Great Britain and the United States, for example by Richard Casey, soon to be External Affairs Minister, in an article in the Melbourne Argus.

Contemporary commentators were not, however, unaware of this neglect of discussion on foreign affairs and often expressed regret over the inevitability of the situation. An editorial in the *Sydney Morning Herald* of August 4, 1943, typifies the sentiment:

To thoughtful people whose hopes are centred upon a lucid approach to post-war conditions, the election campaign so far must be a little discouraging … concerning the mass impulse to escape from the little present to a better future there is strange silence. For constructive pronouncements on the practical questions of Australia's concern in the peace conference, our interest in air communications, and the policy of the Government in international currency and commerce in the post-war era, the electors listen in vain …

This apathy and neglect was not an election

phenomenon but was consistent with the lack of interest shown in foreign affairs during the inter-election periods. Though international news was given wide coverage in the press, debate and discussion did not follow accordingly. This reinforced the trend whereby, as already mentioned, formulation of policy was taking place from above and flowing downward. This, in turn, had a significant effect on the type of policy followed.

Foreign affairs, then, were not central to the winning or losing of elections, nor to the overall debates which took place.

Nevertheless, despite what has been said above, issues were raised by various participants, and policies were debated. The danger exists that because the following pages concentrate on foreign and defence policy the impression may be gained that such policy held a predominant place in the minds of those concerned with the campaigns. This was not the case.

CHAPTER 1
EARLY THINKING ON POST-WAR INTERNATIONAL AFFAIRS: THE 1943 CAMPAIGN

WHEN, on September 3, 1939, the Australian Prime Minister, R.G. Menzies, announced that a state of war existed between Australia and Germany the explanation he gave was based on his concept of the "indivisible Crown", which precluded the King being at war and at peace simultaneously, and couched in terms which expressed the closeness of the relationship between Great Britain and Australia;

… in consequence of a persistence by Germany in her invasion of Poland, Great Britain has declared war upon her and that, as a result, Australia is also at war … There can be no doubt that where Great Britain stands there stand the people of the entire British world.

Australian foreign and defence policy had not, up to this point, followed British policy totally blindly. There had been protests and initiatives and calls for greater consultation on Australia's part, but, generally considered, Australian diplomacy had worked in the shadow of Britain's seniority.

Ironically, despite the "automatic" nature of Australia's entry into hostilities, it was many of the situations created by the second World War which hastened Australia's emergence as a more independent international entity. As W.J. Hudson put it in 1967 in his introduction to *Towards a Foreign Policy: 1914-1941*:

> *The return of Labor to office ... as well as the advent of new personalities and new external situations ... did so much to launch Australia in the 1940s into a full-fledged energetic and utterly independent diplomacy.*

Even before the Labor Party had come to power, however, the Menzies Government had established a precedent by sending R.G. Casey as Australian Minister to Washington in March, 1940, and had followed this by the appointments of Australian Ministers to Tokyo (Sir John Latham) in August, 1940, and to Chungking (Sir Frederic Eggleston) in July, 1941.

It was also under Menzies that the first sketching of ideas about post-war reconstruction took place: though this was largely confined in the early stages to immediate political propaganda and morale requirements. Paul Hasluck, who was External Affairs Minister from 1964 to 1969 and an accomplished historian, put it in another way, writing in 1954:

> *The Australian Government had to counter the notions spread by some political factions that this was just another 'imperialistic' war, that it had been plotted by 'capitalistic war-mongers', and that 'the workers'*

would pay for it in post-war distress. So we heard a good deal in 1940 about the better world that would come after the war.

Various committees were set up in Government departments to consider post-war problems both before and after Labor assumed office. Members of these committees at first concentrated mainly on economic questions but the field of interest soon broadened. Such deliberations were, naturally enough, restricted to departmental officers but as the war situation grew less critical Ministerial attention increased. By 1943, then, much basic groundwork had been completed for further development of this discussion of post-war international relations at both higher and lower levels. The debate which took place during the election campaign of that year did not assume the character it did by sheer chance. It had a definite place in the preliminary airing of post-war concepts.

*

The Sixteenth Parliament of Australia was dissolved on July 7, 1943, to contest the general election which had been set for August 21.

The immediate threat to Australian security brought about by the Japanese sweep south seemed to have passed. Yet there remained many stark reminders that the war was far from over. Japanese forces were still entrenched in New Guinea and the Solomon Islands only a few hundred miles from Australia on what had previously been Australian territory. Most of Europe was still under German occupation.

It was not a false optimism that turned Australian eyes towards the future and peace. There was general accord that the Labor Government had geared the nation for maximum military effect and that Allied victory was merely a matter of time (plus a certain amount of suffering). Serious criticism of the ALP's leadership was almost non-existent, and the Opposition parties in any case were in confused disarray. One contemporary commentator, Warwick Fairfax, expressed the position in this way:

Not, of course, that the war had ceased to matter, but the crisis was regarded as having passed, and the war effort as pretty well organised and as running fairly smoothly of its own momentum.

The perilous state in which Australia had found herself in 1942, however, had a marked effect on the direction which early thinking on post-war arrangements would take. The absolute need for American assistance and the obvious over-extension of British power, so controversially expressed by Curtin and so dramatically driven home by events, gradually loomed larger in all general planning for future defence. British Imperial sentiment vied with a growing awareness of the realities of Britain's situation to force a reconsideration of the place Australia held with respect to the British Empire and the Pacific area – the geopolitical imperative.

The close co-operation which had marked the prosecution of the war by the Allies, and the horrors of war itself, led members of all parties to begin formulating ideas on the extension of this collaboration into the post-war world in order to build upon it a system of collective security whereby such horrors would never again occur. On the other hand, to men like Evatt, there were some ominous indications, exposed by wartime international relations, of dangers inherent in focusing power in the hands of a small number of nations. Evatt's wartime manoeuvres to secure more Australian influence over the course of the war effort, more importance for the Pacific war, and more weapons for Australia began overlapping into his thoughts on the position of such "middle powers" as Australia in the post-war structure.

It should be kept in mind, then, that thoughts on the post-war settlement began to take shape while hostilities were still being waged. There was an intense desire for a peace which would be enduring and for an Australia which would be totally secure from the threat of another attack. The stage was set for an election campaign in which embryonic views of Australia's post-war foreign and defence policies could first be presented for widespread debate and from which the general shape of opposing ideas could emerge. These ideas were necessarily vague and imprecise (and no doubt sometimes as yet even unformed), but they composed the bulk of discussion which took place on future external relations, and pointed towards a much wider and more sophisticated debate to take place over the next few years. As Warwick Fairfax put it in the *Sydney Morning Herald* editorial on the eve of the election:

The time has now come again when the Government must look more directly at Australia's responsibilities to Great Britain and the Empire, and her work, diplomatic and industrial, in the reconstruction of a post-war world, which should be work not only for herself but for others, for humanity, and for world peace.

Early in 1943 Evatt and Curtin began to set the tone of the campaign debate. While overseas campaigning for Australia and the Pacific, Evatt began applying his thoughts to the security of the region to which Australia was inextricably bound, to the idea of a universal security arrangement, and to the part Australia, as a co-belligerent, was to have in the shaping of the peace. The concept of the "arc of islands to the north and north-east" which was later to become a basic principle of defence planning was first put forward as a positive proposal. As yet, however, the significance of the area depended merely on "who should live in, develop, and control it" and on its self-evident "crucial importance" to Australian security, as Evatt said in an address to the Overseas Press Club in New York in April. In a similar way Evatt was claiming the right for the smaller powers to be heard in the peace settlement, justifying the claim by referring to the fact that they may have "something of value to contribute". The problem of security was a universal one, Evatt reminded the world in a BBC broadcast in June, and added portentously: "They reckon ill who leave the Pacific out of account". Evatt was in fact renewing his old battles in the context of peace, but the terms were very uncertain and the reaction to them in Australia was an unknown factor.

Meanwhile, on the home front, Curtin indicated that he too was aware of the problems to be faced in the Pacific. In his speech in support of the overseas conscription proposal at the ALP Conference in June, 1943; Curtin also emphasised the security significance of the "islands adjacent to Australia" and, in fact, placed this aspect in importance before cooperation in Empire defence.

"This land", he said, "may remain free only by Australia remaining the policeman in the Pacific". Or perhaps, as it was later put by Prime Minister John Howard, the US's "deputy sheriff", promoted by George Bush in 2003 to full "sheriff"?

It was a position which, no doubt, Curtin assumed for the particular purpose of the time, and which he later modified, yet in this statement can be seen the type of defence thinking which would be concentrated on in the months to come.

Apart from a last-minute digression on British Commonwealth affairs by Curtin, future arrangements for the Pacific area undoubtedly became the main Labor foreign and defence policy theme during the campaign. The Opposition, on the other hand, at this stage began to draw attention to the part Australia would play in its partnership with the United States and in its membership of the British Empire. It is evident also that an awareness of the importance of future arrangements in the Pacific was growing and broadening within the community. The *Sydney Morning Herald,* in a pre-campaign editorial in July, connected the Pacific theme with the impending predominance of the United States:

… the current of events is bound to draw the Pacific nations closer together. By virtue of her special interests and her immense resources, the United States

must assume the leadership in the Pacific in Peace as in the war, and one of the conditions of our survival as a free, white race will be co-operation with her …

In line with this growing awareness, the Tasmanian University Council proposed a lectureship in Pacific Affairs, and the executive of the League of Nations Union, meeting during the campaign on July 21, supported the proposal emphasising that "the position of Australia would be largely influenced after the war by conditions in other Pacific countries …"

Even the newly-formed (and soon to be dissolved) Liberal Democratic Party, a breakaway from the UAP, which, although not winning any seats, polled well in some NSW electorates, expressed an interest in Pacific affairs, rating them in importance with British Empire relations. As one of its spokesmen, G.N. Wills, put it in the closing days of the campaign:

Australia was now ready to take her place in the world of affairs … This could only be done by an exchange of consular staff with other countries, by representation on an Imperial Parliament, and on a Council of Pacific Relations … The Council of Pacific Relations should consist of representatives of nations bordering on the Pacific, and would administer the mandates at present held by Japan.

The language was indeterminate, the proposals sweeping and their practicality highly doubtful, but the Pacific theme was clearly implied. Australia would be expected to play a more positive role in the Pacific area. In October, 1943, a Gallup poll showed 82% of the voting population was in favour of a permanent military alliance between the Empire and the United States after the war. For Evatt, the signs were obvious enough and he became the most consistent proponent of Australia's need to act forthrightly in the Pacific during the campaign. Evatt, however, did not arrive from overseas until August, and in the meantime Curtin was preparing the groundwork along lines which would be regularly followed throughout the campaign.

Curtin's first opportunity to make a point came with the delivery of the Opposition's policy speech in Brisbane on July 22 by Arthur Fadden, the minority Country Party Leader. It conspicuously made no mention of post-war foreign and defence policy. This omission was, in fact, not in line with standard Opposition policy. William Hughes, nominal leader of the United Australia Party after Menzies' resignation, for instance, was a well-known and staunch advocate of the strengthening of Imperial ties and defence co-ordination after the war. It certainly found no favour with Menzies who had indicated by earlier statements that he believed the greatest problems that would face Australia after the war would be international in nature: The day after Fadden's speech, Menzies delivered his opening address in Camberwell in his own constituency of Kooyong and repeated his conviction that some form of collective security was needed if peace were to be permanent. Later on in the campaign he was to expand this idea to include arrangements with the British Empire and the United States.

Curtin replied from Canberra to Fadden's policy speech immediately, sensing that political advantage could be gained if the Government highlighted the contrast between its forward-looking policy for the peace (even if the points were rather vague), and the complete lack of thinking on the part of the Opposition:

A notable omissions from Fadden's speech was the future policy Australia should follow in the Pacific … If Mr. Fadden's parties are to ignore the islands of the Pacific, economically and defensively, then the charge of isolation lies at their door, not at my Government's.

Nor was Curtin to allow himself to make the same mistake in the ALP policy speech which he delivered three days later, again from Canberra, for, as *The Sydney Morning Herald* commented the next day, "he showed that his Government was thinking deeply about the future of Australia in the Pacific". The reference to post-war international affairs was brief, but it sufficiently reflected the way the Government, Curtin and Evatt especially, was thinking. After mentioning the value of mutual discussion of problems with other members of the British Commonwealth, a point on which he would elaborate late in the campaign, Curtin went on to speak the following day of the need for an effective system of security applicable to the "Pacific and Asiatic zones", although toning down the "policeman of the Pacific" concept to one merely of involvement:

... we feel that the problems of the Pacific and South-East Asia are of special interest to Australia, and are problems in the solution of which Australia has an important contribution to make.

From this point in the campaign, the initiative for the little discussion there was on post-war foreign and defence policy remained entirely with the Labor Party leaders, countered only by a few feeble gestures from Menzies. Evatt returned from abroad in early August and introduced into the discussions two new concepts of post-war policy: that of full employment as an international goal, a concept he was later to pursue with zeal in oversea councils; and that of Asia as a huge, potential market for Australian trade. "Our great opportunity", he said at a press conference on his arrival, "was to provide industrial leadership in the South-West Pacific, where there was already a population of 130 millions."

Evatt repeated this last point when he came to open his own campaign in the Barton electorate, three days later in Hurstville, in the midst of a barrage of reiterated generalities from Curtin and himself on Australia's future interests in the Pacific area:

The opportunities for expansion of our industries in the areas [to our north), and also in Asia will be almost limitless. Once relieved of Japanese domination the many millions of people in these areas will look to Australia just as we shall look to those areas for new markets for our own Australian products.

But the ideas expressed here by Evatt were not in the mainstream of the campaign debate. Curtin summarised the real drift of discussion (and at the same time displayed the kind of generalisations which were being so freely used) at a civic reception for Evatt the day after his return:

Australia must now be prepared to play her part with other great nations in the future of the Pacific and for the preservation of civilisation. The part Australia had played in this war would ensure that its representatives would be heard with respect in the councils of the British Empire and of the Great Powers.

Evatt, in his opening speech, also reverted to and expanded on the defence theme, giving an indication of those countries which he envisaged coming into the zone of interest of the "new Britannia in the Pacific", albeit with a heavily colonial, and obsolescent, burden of responsibility. It was certain, he said,

… that our Pacific responsibilities and interests will be greatly expanded as a consequence of victory … the arc of islands north of us from which Japan has launched so many attacks must be secured against further aggression. Arrangements will be made with such Powers as Holland, Portugal and France, as well as with Britain and the United States, in order to establish a great South-west Pacific zone of security against aggression.

Evatt repeated these points in full in an article written for *The Daily Telegraph* (Sydney) and published three days before the poll adding only two more points: that the welfare of the "natives" in the north would be of utmost concern to Australia, and stressing more forcefully the co-operation which would be necessary with Great Britain, "because we are trustees of British civilization in this part of the world". Obviously, however, there was yet no awareness of the fact that the post-war situation in South-east Asia was in no ways to be so completely dominated by colonial powers as it was before the war – or, at least, it was thought that the Australian public was not yet ready for such a frightening realisation – and that the attitudes of the French, the Portuguese, the Dutch, and even the British, would not be as significant as they once were for Australian security arrangements.

In this speech Evatt also, by talking of the advantages of an all party approach to many matters of foreign policy, pandered somewhat to the fairly widely supported interests promoting a "national" Government:

[The success of the Advisory War Council] illustrates how desirable it is that the representatives of Australia in the conferences dealing with peace terms and Allied problems should not be confined to the representatives of the particular Government in power … Most of these great problems involving industrial expansion and international action, would have nothing whatever to do with party issues … They were exclusively of national concern.

Many, including Fadden, were quick to pick this up, and Evatt was later forced to openly repudiate his supposed support for a "national" Government.

Meanwhile, undoubtedly daunted by the Labor leaders' broad sweep of ideas on the post-war world, and hindered by the fact that the latter's policies were clearly finding favour with the electorate, Menzies and Fadden devoted little time to post-war foreign and defence policy. Menzies, however, was treading warily on ground which he would cover with more determination and more confidence in the years to come. It was not that he considered future international affairs to be of no consequence: quite the contrary. "Everything we stand for", he said in New Norfolk, Tasmania, ten days before the election, developing what he had said to students at the University of Adelaide a few days previously, "depends on the post-war world, and we must make our contribution towards obtaining what we want."

The position which he assumed was as yet an unsophisticated and disjointed one, attempting to connect, as it did, his belief in the need for some form of collective security and the maintenance of the close relationships existing with the United States and Great Britain. He went on:

… we want collective security on a realistic basis. There are two groups which are not likely in any circumstances to make war – the British Empire and the United States. I should start with these two great groups of nations, which have common instincts about peace and war and speak the same language. If we say once and for all that, come rain or shine, those nations will stand or fall on the issues of war and peace we shall put up a most formidable barrier to aggression by other nations.

Fadden confined himself almost exclusively to domestic issues. While in Brisbane, three days before the election, he briefly mentioned some specific defence proposals which indicated a complete lack of any depth of thinking on broad changes which would take place in Asia after the war. Singapore was to be re-established as a naval base, this time with "adequate" air and land defences. If possible it was to become the United Nations' base "to maintain and keep law and order in the Pacific". Universal military training was also to be restored. Fadden's proposals seemed to cause little comment, at least in the southern states.

*

The highlight of the campaign, as far as post-war international affairs was concerned, came in the form of little more than a digression which Curtin made on British Commonwealth affairs while speaking to the United Commercial Travellers Association in Adelaide a week before the poll. It received fairly widespread and favourable publicity, and it left the Opposition totally silent in reply (although Fadden did manage the next day to point out the irony of Curtin's refusal to join a National Government while proposing "a supreme unified Government for the British Empire").

Curtin followed up his thoughts on the subject in the post-election period, and though the proposals were to founder once applied to international realities, it gained Curtin somewhat of a reputation as an Empire theorist – a tag which, of course, was quite advantageous at the time.

Possibly Curtin was prompted by the fact that Menzies was playing strongly on the Imperial theme as a basis for future Australian strategy. He certainly sensed the intense feeling in favour of close cooperation with other Empire countries which continued unabated throughout the war period, and felt it could be applied profitably to post-war appeals. This digression also had the further effect of stimulating preliminary ideas about a post-war international organization. Curtin's proposals hinged on the extension into the peace of the close consultation and collaboration which had taken place during the war. His principal suggestion was the establishment of a standing consultative body with facilities for speedy communication and easy meeting. As the *Sydney Morning Herald* commented:

If the ideas he expressed do not surprise by their novelty, they will certainly, on account of their source and timing, provoke thought on a subject of first importance to British peoples. How far are our common affairs to be managed after the war?

If close consultation among British Empire countries during the war could lead to closer integration after the war, then a similar arrangement could be made for all Allied nations. Curtin, acting quickly on the favourable reaction to his Adelaide speech, followed it up with this proposal in Perth the day after:

I feel that it is desirable that the experience we have had in this war in international consultation is so valuable that the things that will be left after the war will also call for consultation and decision by those who will be speaking for nations as groups. Such an arrangement would call for some machinery which would enable the governments of the different Allied nations to have the opportunity of stating at a conference table their views to influence other governments, not to abrogate their sovereignty, but to hammer out solutions …

Two weeks after the elections, in an issued statement from Canberra, Curtin elaborated on his Empire Consultative Council idea. He had in mind an "ambulatory" permanent representative council, meeting regularly in the capital city of each of the member nations in turn. There would also be a permanent secretariat attached to the council. Curtin repeated his suggestions the next day while still in Canberra, at the same time explaining why he had made them: "I want to develop a practical fraternity among the constituent members of the Empire in their dealings with the world at large and among themselves."

He put his ideas again in a speech to the triennial Federal ALP Conference in December, 1943, in Canberra, but by that time the October Moscow Declaration had evoked visions of a post-war organisation which were beginning to over-shadow Labor's ideas on the British Commonwealth. In fact, Curtin's speech itself indicated how he believed the British Commonwealth could be made an integral part of the larger organisation:

Co-operation between the members of the British Commonwealth for their common interests was closely akin to the principle of regional collaboration between neighbours. If, therefore, Britain, Australia, Canada, and New Zealand, were to develop an understanding about a common policy on their mutual interests in the Pacific, it was equally logical that they should collaborate in a regional organisation with other nations which had parallel interests in this region. Regional arrangements were an essential component of world organisation.

The July-August, 1943, election campaign was, naturally enough, not one which produced a mass of discussion on post-war international policy. The election did, however, provide a forum for the first uneasy testing of very general intimations on the subject of the place Australia would take in the world at peace. There could be no fierce debate between differing viewpoints because any differences were not as yet clearcut enough even to the apologists themselves. In fact, the basic principles around which contemporary thinking revolved, were, in a general way, common to the articulate members of most groups who were involved: more consultation and closer collaboration with the British Empire, especially Britain itself; the need for regional co-operation, with an emphasis on the participation of the United States; the establishment of some form of international security organisation to maintain peace; and most importantly, the expansion of Australian influence in the Pacific for military, economic, political and cultural reasons. All these vague concepts were almost universally accepted as prerequisites for further post-war planning. While planning, in fact, remained in the realm of such theory there was little basis for disagreement. It was only later, when that planning had advanced and become practice, that opposition was aroused on matters of priorities, method and emphasis. The editor of *The Daily Telegraph* (Sydney), Brian Penton, in summing up the election, was able to pick the imprecise nature of most of the points made, and in turn posed several problems for finer definition:

Neither [party] touches the difficult problem of our relation to Asia. What, realistically, is to be our relation to the Empire and to America? On that point, too, the parties are vague. Are we again to depend on a system of imperial defence which becomes inoperative in a crisis because Britain is at that moment up against it herself? Or are we to rely on America? Large brave words about imperial solidarity and friendship with America are no answer to issues complicated by distance, geography and the imminence of an underprivileged and awakening Asia.

These were relevant questions and required detailed explanations and open discussion, but it was perhaps too much to expect such responses at such an early date. *The Bulletin* saw it much the same way on August 25:

Apart from some vague generalities, this aspect of the huge problems ahead was shunned like the plague in the late electioneering. So was the question of Australia's security. Dr. Evatt was a striking Labor exception. Stating that after the war Australia must take its part in protecting the security of the Pacific …

Alan Watt claims in his *The Evolution of Australian Foreign Policy, 1938-1965* that the Cairo Conference of November, 1943, was the catalyst of Australian thinking on post-war organisation. In Paul Hasluck's opinion as he wrote in 1954 in *Australia and the Formation of the United Nations* it was the reports of the exchanges of views leading to the Moscow Declaration which acted as "the real impetus towards political examination of (such) questions." Whatever the case, there is no doubt that such thinking was forged in the immediate and confronting crucible of an all-threatening war in the Asia-Pacific region, finally recognised as Australia's "doorstep".

*

And so the campaign came to its conclusion. As *The Bulletin* – "Australia for the White Man" – summed it up on August 25 with its usual touch of bile yet also a dollop of truth:

Launched by a lie, carried through in a war-overcast atmosphere thick with a smoke barrage of false claims and false issues, an inspiration for narrow provincialism and rowdiness at election meetings, the campaigning for the election of Australia's Seventeenth Parliament laid bare one thing above all – the paucity of men of outstanding ability in each of the parties. … From opening lie till the last day before radio silence was mercifully enforced, the old parties made it an exposing orgy of party politics. The evident leading assumption was that the whole electorate was inhabited by political illiterates.

The general election took place as scheduled on August 21 and resulted in a convincing win for John Curtin and his Labor Party Government. The ALP secured around 58% of the preferred vote, a swing of about 8% in its favour from the previous 1940 election which had been more or less a dead heat.

The overwhelming victory was as much a consequence of the electorate wanting stability in the wartime crisis, and recognising the fact that the Curtin Government had achieved considerable success in the management of that crisis and the waging of the war, as it was of the total disarray of their opposition. Billy Hughes had succeeded Robert Menzies after the latter's resignation as leader of the majority United Australia Party but had not assumed the leadership of the Opposition which had fallen to Arthur Fadden of the Country Party. Nor did he assume leadership of the Opposition campaign during the election which did nothing to enhance the Opposition's legitimacy as a potential Government. He resigned as leader a month after the election and three days before his 81st birthday. Robert Menzies re-took the leadership and so heralded the arrival of a new era in Australian politics, though it would take a little more time to come to fruition.

Meanwhile John Curtin, Herb Evatt and the Labor Government would get down to prosecuting the war, and preparing for the peace.

CHAPTER 2
IMMEDIATE POST-WAR IDEALISM
THE DISCUSSION BLOSSOMS:
THE 1946 CAMPAIGN

THE three years between the August election of 1943
and the dissolution of the Seventeenth Parliament
on August 16, 1946, and the subsequent election
on September 9, witnessed dramatic changes on
both the international and domestic scenes. The
war in Europe hurried to a close, quickly followed
by the war in the Pacific. Atomic weapons were
introduced as an additional complication in
the settlement of international crises. Imminent
victory brought the establishment of the United
Nations Organisation, and peace concluded the
wartime alliance of the United States, the USSR
and Great Britain, precipitating the confrontation,
which gradually grew more apparent, between
the "Soviets" and the "West". Britain was forced to
turn its attention to the inevitable disintegration of
Empire, in particular independence for India.

More withdrawals from colonial possessions
also seemed inevitable. In January, 1946, the
first United Nations General Assembly met, and
two months before the election the Paris Peace
Conference opened with Evatt representing
Australia. More specific issues arose when

fighting flared up between Arabs, Jews and British soldiers in Palestine, and when Indonesian nationalists proclaimed a Republic on August 17, 1946, in opposition to the returning Dutch colonial administration. All these matters affected Australia, Australian policy, and most importantly, Australian attitudes in one way or another.

On the homefront, significant political changes also occurred. By the elections of 1946, two new leaders were confronting each other. Menzies had taken over as Leader of the Opposition from Fadden by assuming the leadership of the newly-formed Liberal Party which had superseded the disintegrated United Australia Party. Apart from the other obvious advantages this afforded Menzies, it also improved the coverage given to his statements in the press and enhanced their importance.

Menzies remained chief spokesman for the Opposition in international relations, but he was now supported by two new specialists, R.G. Casey and P.C. Spender, both very able and with widespread reputations.

Casey had been Governor of Bengal since 1944 and previous to that had served as U.K. Minister of State in the Mid-East, member of the British War Cabinet, First Australian Minister to the United States, and Federal Treasurer, 1935–39.

Spender had been Federal Member for

Warringah since 1937 and had served as a Minister several times, including a period as Treasurer in 1940, and had sat on the Advisory War Council, 1940-1945. Early in 1944, he had written, and had privately printed, a booklet entitled, *Australia's Foreign Policy: The Next Phase*. In it his well-balanced argument is concentrated on an attack on Evatt's lack of the "dynamic of future". He does reserve some praise for Evatt's break with conservative patterns of foreign policy, and he is not always thinking along similar lines as Menzies. His own emphasis is on Australia as a Pacific nation – its advantage and exposure as such. In his plea for action to gain practical advantage for Australia's interests, as opposed to Evatt's preferred "faith in the written word", can be seen the germ of some of his later work as Minister for External Affairs: "First and foremost", he says, "Australia is a Pacific power ... The geographical facts point to a strategic link with the US as one of the most important imperatives in Australia's foreign policy ... "

These two men added depth and diversity to the Opposition's case and weight to the attack.

On the Government's side, Chifley had taken over the Prime Ministership following Curtin's death in 1945. Chifley was not as outspoken, or, at least, not as publicly committed, on foreign policy as was his predecessor. However, it is not so certain that he was so aloof as "to let his Minister for External Affairs, Evatt, take the lead", even if it was "within understood bounds", as L.F. Crisp wrote in his biography of Chifley in 1963. Chifley did have definite ideas on foreign and defence policy, and it is more likely that he put these into effect, when he felt it necessary, either through personal contact, or by such means as his own officers in the Prime Minister's Department, as Greenwood and Harper suggest. Nevertheless, the dominating personality of the period in the field of foreign affairs was undoubtedly Evatt. His natural abilities and personal inclinations combined with the peculiar circumstances of the time allowed him to take full advantage of his position. During the period 1943-1946, Evatt's ideas on an international organisation and international affairs crystallised, and he lost no opportunity in presenting these ideas to a wide-ranging public.

The very general lines along which post-war foreign policies were being shaped by various sections of the Australian public continued to be discussed throughout the period, but, apart from these, three specific issues caused particular debate: the Australia-New Zealand Agreement, the San Francisco Conference and the inauguration of the United Nations, and the crisis in the Netherlands East Indies with the accompanying controversy over the trade union ban on Dutch ships in Australian waters. The last-mentioned issue, however, was the only one which brought about any marked differences in opinion, though the Australia-New Zealand Agreement and United Nations policy contained the seeds of an ever-widening difference in approaches to international affairs in general.

The Agreement between Australia and New Zealand was signed in Canberra on January 21, 1944. It appears to have been provoked to some measure by a growing concern, on the part of Evatt especially, over "Great Power" disregard for smaller nations' views, especially following the various meetings of leaders of the major Allied nations. It was, in fact, a statement of initiative in Pacific affairs. Future joint action in foreign affairs and defence arrangements on the part of Australia and New Zealand was hardly the type of issue which would have split Australian public opinion. It was in fact of such little interest that it was not included in any public opinion polling of the period.

The little criticism which the treaty brought upon the Government was aimed, not at the intent, but at the terms in which it was expressed. The debate in Parliament on Evatt's tabling of the Agreement and his Ministerial statement of February 10, 1944, was the main forum for criticism on this occasion. Argument revolved around two main Opposition points: firstly, that the Agreement offended Australia's allies by overstating rights which were not being questioned, and secondly, that it unnecessarily pointed out the obvious. Senator MacDonald put the Opposition's case in this way:

Nothing we do should endanger our future relations with Great Britain and the United States of America. Australia, and even New Zealand, are only inviting trouble by entering into such pacts without consultation, first of all, with our stronger friends, Great Britain and the United States of America. We are deliberately provoking retaliation on the part of our allies by entering into such agreements ...

The Government's case in reply hinged on the claims that the Agreement actually strengthened British Commonwealth ties, that it improved Australia's chances of being effective in international councils, and that it was crucial to Australian interests that it take initiatives in the post-war Pacific settlement. What public reaction there was tended to agree. *The Sydney Morning Herald's* editorial praised the agreement, adding only one qualification:

However energetically we and the New Zealanders develop our peace-keeping armaments, we and our small neighbours will still have to rely for security primarily upon the might of the United States and Britain. That chastening reflection should make us wary of appearing too importunate in our claims or pretentious in our ambitions.

That "pretentiousness" which was detected in the document, was later to become one of the apparent characteristics of Evatt's approach to foreign affairs and which would come under heavy attack.

The debate over the United Nations was far more prolonged and widespread, and was more central to the overall assumptions on foreign policy which were developing. There was little division over the issue for there was almost universal support for the idea of an international organisation to keep the peace, with the use of armed force if necessary. A Gallup Poll in July, 1944, had two-thirds supporting a world league having an armed force, and a year later 70% wanted Australia to contribute to that force. Nevertheless, a Gallup Poll taken immediately after the San Francisco Conference found that only one third of the population were interested in the proceedings and by August, 1945, this had dropped to just over a quarter, of whom about 80% felt Australia should support the Charter. Ratification by Parliament took just eight sitting days to pass through all its stages.

However, as time went by the scepticism and dissatisfaction grew, and this was especially so on the part of the Opposition, who were always inclined to the view that the British Commonwealth was a more trustworthy association to which to belong. The idea of close co-operation between the British Commonwealth and the United States as a basis for further co-operation also found more favour with them. As Spender put it:

... whilst an effective world union may not be capable of being rapidly achieved, an English-speaking association comprising the British Commonwealth and the United States is something within our power.

On the other hand, Evatt's ideas were clear. He believed in the United Nations as a potentially effective means for, firstly, "the maintenance of world peace", and secondly, "the promotion of economic and social welfare". To a great degree Evatt's ability and enthusiasm carried the rest of the Government with him, though, of course, his appeals fell on very receptive ears. All this is not to say that the Opposition had a monopoly over policy advocating co-operation with the British Commonwealth and the United States. The Government also emphasised this aspect of policy both in practice and in public broadcasting. *The Sydney Morning Herald* probably caught the tenor of the country best when it said: "However much we may trust in the new League, we must in future keep our powder dry."

Towards the end of 1945 an entirely new issue, with several branches involved, joined the debate over foreign policy and remained useful for the Opposition and troublesome to the Government until the latter's electoral defeat in 1949. The cause of the dispute, the independence movement in the Netherlands East Indies, received the tacit support of the Government, in the name of regional stability, and the disapproval of the Opposition, supposedly on the grounds that independence would be premature. However, more significant, simply because it was nearer home, was the ban imposed by several unions on Dutch ships in Australian waters.

This ban, which the Government failed to suppress, provided the Opposition with several avenues of attack all of which commanded considerable sympathy with the electorate: betrayal of the Dutch as a wartime ally, the connection between the rebel leaders and the Japanese, loss of trade, weakening of defence contact, and the dictating of a Government's foreign policy by "undemocratic" means. Even the reluctance to act on the part of the Government was exploited. "No attempt has been made by the Government," Menzies said in Parliament, "to expound or to enforce any policy …

that runs counter to the views of a few Communist-led agitators on the waterfront".

The "strange affair of the Dutch ships", as *The Sydney Morning Herald* called it in an article in their "Election Issues" series , was the type of issue which would remain current for some time, not least because it was good electoral material for the Government's critics. In fact, Menzies made it clear in his policy speech to open the Oppositon's election campaign, again from Camberwell in his seat of Kooyong on August 20, 1946, that they were not about to allow one aspect, especially the minority control of Australia's foreign policy, become a "dead" issue. "The Government's inaction was, he said, "supine surrender to a minority of communists and agitators." This set the tone for many years to come.

Nevertheless, the election campaign was, once again, to provide little debate over foreign and defence policy, even though the number of subjects out of which issues could be produced had increased markedly since 1943, and despite pleas from certain quarters:

In the present electoral campaign it is disquieting that little has been said by many of the candidates about where they stand regarding the most important question that confronts Australia and the world today – the task of making a success of U.N.

Mud Map to AUKUS

(R.R. Garran President of the United Nations Association.)

There are two broad explanations for this neglect. Firstly, there were so few differences between the parties that the Opposition felt no worthwhile distinguishing impression could be made on the electorate on a widespread basis. As the *Sydney Morning Herald* put it shortly after the election:

Basically, no doubt, the Government, and the Opposition do have the same outlook on foreign relations. The tendency in present circumstances is for differences less of substance than of emphasis to be exaggerated in the course of debate, the Opposition deeming it to be its duty to make a show of criticism …

Additionally, it became obvious as the campaign progressed, that Evatt was maintaining his popularity – mention of his name by Chifley for example evoking applause from audiences – his policies were being well received even amongst otherwise unsympathetic media observers, and that no useful purpose could thus be served for the Opposition by highlighting foreign affairs.

Even *The Bulletin* on August 25 could find no fault:

Dr. Evatt returned in the midst of these babblings and ravings from his mission abroad. He had a done a good job, and hence had more cause to feel sure of himself than any other of his party.

Secondly, the crucial issues of the campaign were unmistakably domestic, focusing on taxation and industrial unrest (hence the use by the Opposition of the ban on Dutch shipping mainly in the context of domestic considerations).

Such issues, therefore dominated the electioneering, believing that foreign affairs would be irrelevant to the outcome of the election and consequently time-wasting, although the Government used Evatt and his policies as a vote-catcher to some degree. As Professor F.A. Bland of the University of Sydney and leader of the committee which was supporting a "No" vote at the referendum being held simultaneously with the general election, and later to be elected to the House of Representatives for the Liberals, lamented:

While elections in Australia continue to be fought at the bread-and-butter level, matters such as defence, foreign affairs, and tariff policy go by default …

Because Evatt was in Paris at the Peace Conference and did not arrive in Sydney – to general acclaim for his work there – until August 29, the Government's case received little attention till that date. Chifley, however, had made a very early tour of Western Australia, and though defence and foreign policy did not feature, his speeches hinted at the types of points which would later be stressed at more length. The issues he touched on were in no way unusual or unexpected. In broad outline they included the twin bases of British Empire co-operation and a successful and effective United Nations; the need for a strong security system which would protect an exposed Australia whose safety in isolation had been "obliterated" by the "advances of science", and the personal standing of Evatt, as *The West Australian* editorialised:

... Dr. Evatt had played an important part not only at the Paris Conference but also in the foundation work associated with the U.N.O at San Francisco ... It was essential that there should be a complete system of Empire defence with the closest liaison between the Dominions and the United Kingdom ...

The points were very briefly made, and the silence which ensued for the next two weeks could be interpreted as indicative of the confidence which the Government held in the successful public reception of its foreign and defence policy, as well as evidence supporting the belief that foreign affairs had become the personal territory of Evatt and lapsed while he was away. Indeed this criticism of Evatt's proprietorial dominance of the field grew in intensity as time went by, becoming in itself an important factor in the general foreign affairs debate

Meanwhile, in the intervening period before Evatt returned, and taking advantage of his absence, the Opposition launched its most substantial and trenchant attack on Government policies and put forward its own alternatives (though criticism took the greater share by far of the comments). Menzies and Spender took the lead for the Opposition, Menzies setting out in his policy speech, once again delivered from his electorate of Kooyong, the main points which would be made throughout the campaign.

While most emphasis was on tax reduction and what might be described as "national development", Menzies also attacked the Government's failure to act on the Dutch ships embargo, claiming that the breakdown of "political and trading relations" was an outcome of this negligence. He emphasised the need for a closely integrated Empire and Imperial defence structure including a "united British Empire policy and voice" in international affairs, an acceptance on Australia's part of a greater share in armament and munitions production for the whole Empire, and improved defence forces. There was, of course, the usual mention of universal military conscription, a controversy which, however, in no way became an issue in the campaign. Evatt's monopoly of the foreign affairs sphere and the lack of parliamentary discussion on it Menzies found "disturbing", and he called for an all-party Parliamentary Standing Committee on

Foreign Affairs to counteract the tendency, raising such a proposal for the first time more as a tactical move than as a real possibility, it can be imagined. There was no mention whatsoever of the United Nations, of the Pacific or South-east Asian security areas, and the only reference to co-operation with the United States was in a very incidental phrase expressing Australia's need for "powerful friends and allies". Menzies clearly believed that the Government's foreign policy could not be successfully attacked to any marked degree, and its rather formal inclusion in the Liberal platform was more to indicate that the Opposition had at least some alternative, however slight.

Speaking in various locations around the country during the ensuing campaign Menzies did not elaborate in depth on the points he made, and once Evatt had returned appears to have completely dismissed foreign affairs as an electoral handicap for the Opposition by not referring to it again except in passing Three days after his Kooyong speech he repeated his argument that Australian foreign policy with regard to the Netherlands East Indies had been dictated by "a little gang on the waterfront". A little later in the campaign he maintained that the Opposition, as a Government, would formulate a positive policy towards the situation, though he is no more specific on what such a policy would be. Surprisingly, however, Menzies did not even expand the Imperial theme on which he could have expected to make some ground, except briefly as an example of a "non-experimental" contrast to the "highly experimental" United Nations.

Hughes, still a staunch supporter of Imperial ties, denounced Evatt's methods as breaking up the solidarity of the Empire and claimed that the only assurance of Australia's security lay in its "operating within the Empire as a living force", and in Britain and the United States acting together. Hughes, probably even more than Menzies, considered the power base of international politics as all-important, and hence could not suffer Evatt criticising Britain in any way that might reduce the closeness of the relationship, or, as Hughes put it, making Australia appear as if she were "pawing the ground, trying to find a spot between two camps". Hughes, however, received little publicity, and by this time carried even less weight with the electorate than the little he had during the 1943 campaign.

Even so, it was Hughes who posed a contrary position to Evatt in a pair of juxtaposed articles in the *Sydney Morning Herald* four day before election day. This was probably the longest exposition of Opposition foreign policy published during the campaign. The fact that the Opposition's answer to Evatt was written by Hughes, however, must raise the question again of how far other Opposition leaders treated foreign policy as a serious issue, and how much of Evatt's superiority in the public eye they felt they could overcome. Hughes, in the article, attacks Evatt's "lone-wolf tactics" and pleads for integration of Imperial foreign policy and defence arrangements, an eerily prescient position given the recent AUKUS declaration.

Spender, while following the general lines of Opposition policy in his attacks on the Government, was putting forward a far more detailed and specific case, and was broaching new areas untouched by other Opposition supporters. His ideas were similar to those he had expressed in his pamphlet two and a half years previously, though, of course, amended in the light of experience.

He was still aiming his attack predominantly at Evatt, especially Evatt's method, and his gaze still focused on the Pacific and South-east Asian region. Evatt, to Spender, speaking in Sydney, lacked any idea of the essence of the motive in a nation's foreign policy. Evatt remained the man of the written document, of proper procedure, and high-flown phrases, the man whose "fatal tendency" was to "confuse form for substance and to avoid the realities". Evatt applied his talents where they were not producing most use for Australia, no matter how useful they may be for the world. Attention should have been redirected to Australia's north and the "strategic weaknesses that still existed there", he said at Hurstville on August 14. "It is our security in the Pacific which is of supreme importance to us all." Spender saw such security resting only in the increasing solidarity of the "English-speaking nations" he added a week later, and again on August 27:

… without the aid of the British and the United States, Australia had no hope of maintaining its White Australia policy in thirty years time.

So Spender, too, saw Australian security in power-base terms, in terms of the reality of powerful aid from friends and allies, and he believed a nation's foreign policy should actively seek means to ensure this end. In Spender's words, "the Liberal Party believed in the general principles of the United Nations Organisation, but artful diplomacy in Europe and America was not producing results in Australia's best interests", to which Evatt on his return from the Paris Peace Conference on August 30 rather feebly replied, possibly influenced by his sojourn there:

We cannot be isolationist and simply limit our interests to the Pacific. What happens in Europe, for instance the settlement with Finland, has a vital bearing

*on peace, and world wars have an unpleasant habit of
breaking out first of all in remote parts of Europe.*

Spender called for something more precise
than this sort of verbal generalising, and his
comment, that the only value of Evatt's actions
were "to attract world-wide attention to himself"
had a ring of truth about it.

Spender's questioning of the basis of Evatt's
foreign policy was by far the most meaningful
of the campaign, but as yet it could not expect
to receive popular acceptance. For example,
according to a Gallup poll taken in mid-1945 the
population was about evenly divided among
those satisfied, dissatisfied and undecided on the
UN, and the satisfied group had dropped to one-
quarter by mid-1947. On the other hand, Gallup
Poll findings in October, 1943, showed 82% were
in favour of a permanent military alliance between
the Empire and the US after the war.

Later, when the public had lost some
confidence in the United Nations as an effective
international organisation for peace-keeping,
Evatt's approach became far more open and
susceptible to such probing as this.

In the midst of a deluge of newspaper
editorials condemning the Government's
acquiescence in the actions of the waterfront

unions towards Dutch ships, generally in terms of Australia's honour, the threat to commerce, and friendship with the Dutch, and three days after Evatt's return, Chifley delivered the ALP Policy Speech which was broadcast nationally on September 2. In contrast to Menzies' earlier speech, Chifley gave a certain prominence to defence and foreign affairs, again displaying the confidence which the Government held in the popular reception of its policies.

Chifley based the case for the Government's re-election mainly on the strength of past performances, both during and after the war. Similar problems of national development, such as housing, wool and wheat, repatriation and economic balance, were raised as Menzies had done, and similar promises were given. But Chifley began the detailed platform points with an outline of Government defence policy and continued for some time in the same vein. He reiterated, in broad terms, most Labor policy from "enthusiastic and sustained support of the United Nations", to "co-operation in Empire defence", the reciprocal use, in conjunction with the United States, of Pacific bases, the significance of developments in modern warfare for defence planning, and the organisation of Australia's defence forces.

One difference in emphasis between

Labor's policy and that of the Opposition was immediately obvious. The United Nations had taken a predominance in the Government's overall planning which the Opposition could never accept. Measures for Empire defence co-ordination, though necessary and taken for granted, had slipped into a secondary role. In Chifley's words:

The forces we maintain must be related to measures for co-operation in Empire defence. The Government regards this as an arrangement for collective defence, consistent with the purposes and principles of the United Nations. As such it is a contribution to the power and strength of the United Nations.

Justification for Imperial co-operation by reference to the United Nations was truly a remarkable position for an Australian Prime Minister to assume, but a partial explanation appeared when Chifley moved onto the field of "international relationships". It was obvious that the Government still viewed British Commonwealth ties as the sheet anchor of Australian foreign policy, the difference, however, now lying in the nature of those ties. Australia had become the principal British power in the Pacific, and as such its policies had to be more independent, or "distinctive", as Chifley called it. Co-operation was to be on a basis of equality, or rather, Australia was to be the "trustee of British civilisation" in the Pacific. The focus of Australian foreign policy having shifted almost totally to the Pacific area, together with the obvious downgrading of Britain's Pacific power, this entailed a re-orientation of British Commonwealth relations:

Australia's relations with Britain today are, therefore, firmly based on the hard realities of world politics, with Australia not only giving practical expression to her rights, but also assuming and effectively carrying out the heavy responsibilities that belong to her new status. Never has co-operation with Britain been more realistic or more cordially reciprocal ...

Chifley reinforced this emphasis the Government now placed on the Pacific area (including a reference to Japan specifically – one of the very few times Japan is referred to during the campaign, and even more surprising, coming as it did, in a context of trading relationships) by going on to speak of the:

... countries lying to the immediate north of Australia ... thousand million people, whose living standards, if increased only by a fraction, would establish a market for all that Australia could manufacture.

Chifley's Policy Speech was thus an indication of the development which had taken place in foreign policy thinking, and in the public expression of this thinking. No longer talk merely of a defensive "arc of islands" to the north, but a complete broadening of interest in the area to the north of Australia and a desire for wide involvement.

There could be little criticism made of such policy, and the press editorials the following day did not try. The best that could be managed was a poor backhanded compliment by *The West Australian*:

What [Chifley] had to say about Imperial relations and the close co-operation now existing between Britain and Australia merely emphasises the swing of Labor opinion towards Opposition policy – for it was never the Opposition parties who were isolationist.

With Evatt about to embark on detailed explanations of his successful participation in world affairs and the virtues of the United Nations, the Government's foreign policy was virtually unassailable in the circumstances of the election campaign. Such assaults as were made had had their basis undermined by Chifley's expression of faith, however drastically qualified, in British Commonwealth co-operation. Casey, for instance, made no mark when he said: "The Liberal Party intended to strengthen and to integrate further the links that bound British countries", for so too, it seemed, did the Labor Party.

Other voices were raised in protest – such as W.C. Wentworth who called Evatt a "stooge of

Russia's stalling tactics", and T.T. Hollway, future Liberal Premier of Victoria, who called him "a little emperor of a committee representing South American Republics" – mentioned the trade union dictation of foreign policy. Fadden in Bendigo on September 17 talked of how the Government "accepted in toto the policy laid down by the Communist-controlled unions on the waterfront", and how Evatt's flair for publicity had been detrimental to Empire unity. But Labor had gained the initiative and the Opposition could resort only to nuisance attacks, preferring to concentrate on other, more potentially profitable (in an electoral sense) domestic issues.

*

Evatt opened his own campaign for the electorate of Barton at Rockdale on September 3, and in his speech outlined the major points which he would repeat and elaborate, with a few digressions, during the next three and a half weeks of the campaign. His theme was, not unexpectedly, the United Nations, and rather trite phrases were commonplace: "the resolute determination of a young nation", "in the interests of world peace and justice", "our policy of democracy and justice". Evatt's aim was to demonstrate how Australia's best interests were being served by assisting the cause of world peace and international harmony:

Mud Map to AUKUS

Labor's foreign policy is directed not only towards the security and welfare of ourselves but of all peoples. Australia's international obligations are to help establish international machinery for world peace and security and assist international planning of social and economic welfare.

Evatt was also keen to refute any suggestion that his policies were adding to British Commonwealth disunity, stressing a point similar to that which had been made concerning the Australia-New Zealand Agreement, that the strength of the British Commonwealth was directly related to the strength of its constituent members:

While it is a disservice to cloak differences of opinion within the British Commonwealth, there is unity in fundamentals. The separate influence of Australia and other Dominions does not detract from the influence of the whole British Commonwealth, but adds to it.

Opponents of Evatt, in contrast, felt strongly that it was quite wrong to display naked "family" disagreements, to the public gaze, in the least, perhaps even treacherous.

Evatt failed to develop these stated principles during the campaign, but rather tended merely to restate them in different ways. Two additional aspects did arise briefly, however.

Firstly, towards the end of the campaign, in an address on "the Role of Australia in World Affairs" delivered at The University of Western Australia, Evatt appeared to be attempting to justify his outspoken attitude in international councils by referring to the need for Australia to "secure an effective voice and influence". Second, owing perhaps to his neglect of it up until that time, in the last week before the election he switched some of his attention to the specific urgency of Pacific security in accordance with those principles set out in Chifley's policy speech. Yet even here Evatt could not resist associating an issue with the United Nations:

Concentration of Pacific security and on Australian security was not inconsistent with activity in all aspects of the work of the United Nations. Security in the Pacific, and in any other region was dependent upon world security.

On only one occasion was Evatt drawn out by an opponent speaking in the campaign. The issue of Manus Island and the United States base there had been smouldering for some time. However, as yet, there was an atmosphere of uncertainty surrounding it owing to the fact that there had been no final declaration on the outcome of secretive negotiations, and it had not become a "live" issue. A month before the election *The West Australian* ventured an editorial opinion on the subject:

… it would be a colossal piece of foolishness if

Australia were to discourage the establishment and maintenance of a great American defensive base in close proximity to our northern shores.

Three days later, J.P. Abbott, a N.S.W. Country Party Member who had had some official connection during the war with the American forces locally, attacked Evatt for refusing "to hand over Manus Island for fortification by America." The attack was a little premature for negotiations were still underway, as Evatt implied in his firm reply to Abbott speaking in Fairfield, Sydney:

The Government would never consent to handing over one inch of territory that had come under its control. But we are willing for the United States, if she desires, to have use of facilities on Manus if, at the same time, a reciprocal arrangement can be made for the use of facilities in United States territory.

Although the stand Evatt was taking was quite unrealistic, Chifley quickly jumped to his support, claiming from Brisbane the next day that what Evatt had said had the support of Cabinet. But the whole question then lapsed until well after the elections when it was again raised on a much more serious note.

Evatt's statements during the campaign, then, expressed principles that were less of a foreign policy than a philosophy. The occasion was a rare one when he would refer to specific points of policy, and Spender's early question in an address at Mascot, Sydney, on August 22 had much to recommend it: "What, in precise terms, has Evatt done to strengthen Australia's security?" In fact, Chifley's brief participation in the debate on foreign policy could be looked upon as a balance to Evatt's rather indefinite utterances. Chifley, for instance, speaking in Ballarat, stressed the continuing importance of Empire ties along the lines set out in his policy speech as if to make it clear that the Government had not forgotten:

The Government felt it is absolutely fundamental that there should be the closest co-operation between the Englishspeaking peoples of the world. To preserve the strength of the British Empire, more and more responsibility must be carried by the Dominions in the future.

Nevertheless, Chifley and the rest of the Labor Party realised that one of the Government's most valuable assets in the election was Evatt's current personal standing throughout the country – confirmed also by the high (about 67%) personal vote, he received in his electorate of Barton in Sydney – and as the campaign progressed this advantage was fully utilised (such as in the ALP advertisements shown below in the Appendix).

*

Mud Map to AUKUS

The 1946 federal election campaign proved relatively disappointing as a platform for debate on foreign and defence policy, and this was largely due to the Opposition's unwillingness to indulge in argument over a topic by which they could not hope to gain votes. Most issues had a basis of general agreement between opposing parties and were therefore discussed in very general terms. British Commonwealth relations, co-operation with the United States (despite the developing Manus Island diplomatic imbroglio), support for the United Nations, the need for strong Australian defence forces in future, all received almost obligatory attention.

One of the most interesting features of the campaign was the absence of debate on certain issues. Military conscription caused no controversy, and one obvious subject for fruitful discussion, Japan and the Peace Treaty, received scant consideration. The undoubted explanation for this latter disregard was the strong feeling that universally existed throughout the community in favour of a harsh treaty with Japan thus leaving little room for lengthy or significant debate. The topic was also in the realms of diplomatic manoeuvring and had little appeal for popular discussion.

C.W. Frost, the Minister for Repatriation, did

pander to parochial interests while in Hobart by promising to establish an Australian whaling industry, partly on the basis of a factory ship and several chasers to be secured from Japan as reparations Other than this gesture, which was made to calm fears aroused by the announcement that Japanese whaling fleets would again be allowed into the Southern whaling zones and received no publicity beyond Tasmania, issues involving Japan were not explored.

In his final appeal on the eve of the poll, Chifley's first point in the case for the Government's re-election was: "To ensure Australia's security as a partner in the British Commonwealth, and in association with the United States by reciprocal agreement. Neither Menzies nor Fadden in summing up mentioned foreign policy or defence in any way. And when the election had been contested, Evatt could quite confidently claim that one of the three reasons for the Government's success was that the "people had endorsed the foreign policy of the Curtin-Chifley Governments."

*

The 1946 federal election was the first in which the ALP was confronted by a new Liberal Party in coalition with a Country Party, a confrontation that has remained the norm to this day. It was also the first time the ALP won successive elections.

Although the Government suffered a 4% loss in vote its victory was still quite pronounced with about 54% of the preferred vote and a clear majority in the House of Representatives and an almost clean sweep in the Senate. The rejuvenation of a conservative Opposition under Menzies was certainly one cause of its improved electoral result, but the momentum of wartime success justifiably ascribed to the Labor Governments and the desire for a period of stability, including in foreign affairs and defence, after such a period of critical disruption, carried the day.

The popular mood, however, fanned by the conservative forces and underpinned by the surge of communism, was to undergo a seachange in the coming months and years.

CHAPTER 3
THE DETERIORATION IN INTERNATIONAL RELATIONS AS HOPE FADES: THE 1949 CAMPAIGN

THE Eighteenth Parliament of Australia was dissolved on October 31, 1949 and a general election called for December 12. The size of the House of Representatives had been increased from the previous 74 seats to 121 seats, and the Senate consequently from 36 to 60 seats. The situation as it existed in 1946 had altered dramatically by 1949. For one thing, your humble author had been born, although he took no interest in the ensuing campaign at the time, and did not participate in any way. For its part, the Labor Government was to discover that its policies, which had been so advanced in the immediate post-war period, were now thoroughly outmoded. The international situation, as it became more and more critical, played into the hands of the Opposition, whose foreign policy linked up with their domestic anti-communist policies to find increasing sympathy with the Australian public.

The period saw a further development (some would say deterioration) in British Commonwealth relations with the withdrawal of Eire and Burma, and the admission of India as a republic recognising the monarch as a symbol only, a situation which Menzies found "mysterious", and Spender described as based on "strained ambiguities and meaningless phrases".

Ferment in Asia and the Middle East increased apace, and by the end of 1949 a Communist revolutionary Government ruled China, and a Jewish state had been carved out of Palestine. Probably the most significant and ominous events of all, however, were the formation of the Cominform in October, 1947, and the signing of the North Atlantic Treaty in April, 1949.

In Australia, the Liberal Party set about consolidating the small gains it had made in 1946, and perfecting that distinctive anti-Communist policy which it was beginning to use so effectively. The Labor Government found itself faced with crisis after crisis, with strikes periodically paralysing various sections of the nation. In October-November, 1947, Chifley made a classic, and probably fatal, political blunder by attempting to nationalise the banks without sufficient popular preparation or support.

The dominating problem of the period, however, was the situation which became known as the "Cold War", and the eventual realisation of the ineffectiveness of the United Nations as an international security organisation. It had soon become clear that the differences between Russia and the other Allies were serious and irreparable, and it was the consideration of this looming confrontation which finally affected most other aspects of international policy. The Australian public, however, was not quick to react in opposition to Russian bloc policy, much less so than Americans, due in part to the reversal of attitudes which this entailed after the heavy wartime propaganda depicting allied unity. The widespread desire which still existed for an enduring peace based on continued Great Power unity was also reflected in the tardiness of Labor Government critics in expressing strong anti-Russian sentiments. The situation which was now sifting into the national consciousness was gradually to assume an overriding importance by permeating national attitudes of every form.

By the time of the 1946 elections, although the gap between East and West was already wide, the electorate was still not sufficiently favourably sensitive to any policy which may have been heavily based on an anti-Russian conviction, and the Opposition was limited to only sporadic taunts about Evatt's occasional support of Russian viewpoints (although at the same time, Opposition spokesmen were just as ready to criticise Evatt for pretentiously disagreeing with Russia).

During the next three years, however, the mood of the Australian public swung heavily away from favouring conciliation to supporting measures which would contain and frustrate Russian, or Soviet policy, and analogously, further British and American moves.

Opinion polling taken through this period provides a picture of the shifting sands. In February, 1946, one third of the adult population felt the Soviets wanted to dominate the world, but by August, 1946, it was almost half those asked felt the USSR was bent on becoming the ruling world power, and in November, 1947, 61% now believed it was an aggressive nation. Then, by August, 1948, three-quarters of those asked believed the USSR wished to dominate the world, thus more than doubling over only two and a half years. At the same time 58% said they would fight alongside the US against the Soviet Union, and another 15% would assist short of war.

In its most substantial form, this change of mood undermined Evatt's idea of foreign policy with its emphasis on judgements supposedly based purely on the merits of each individual situation. It posed a total conflict of approaches, and Evatt failed to solve the dilemma he was faced with, especially in the eyes of the electorate. He was perpetrating thorough confusion as to motives and interests, and this, in turn, could not help but lower his esteem and his credibility. *The Sydney Morning*

Mud Map to AUKUS

Herald noted in April, 1948, Evatt's faltering when commenting on one of his ministerial statements to the House of Representatives:

The most remarkable feature of a lengthy speech was his success in discussing the extremely perilous state of the world without even once attempting to diagnose the causes of what he himself bluntly termed "the drift to war". His whole speech, indeed, seems to indicate the Government's determination to avoid any criticism of Russia, although most of the impasses and crises which he describes and deplores are directly traceable to one cause alone – Soviet intransigence.

By 1949 even Evatt had been forced to admit that the United Nations had failed as a major international force, but unfortunately for him and the ALP, the public had been left with the legacy of his earlier expressions of faith. Meanwhile, the electorate was becoming more and more attentive to Opposition pleas for a halt in the policy of "appeasement", and for preparation for war. Spender, for instance, found the parallel between Russia and Nazi Germany "alarming". "The world is moving with increasing momentum towards war", he was able to say by early 1948, at Harbord in Sydney.

The failures of the United Nations were important factors in shaping attitudes of the period, and the diminishing hopes in its effectiveness went hand in hand with the growing reliance on the United States which the public increasingly demanded. Indonesia, Palestine, Berlin, Greece – the United Nations was not to be dismissed entirely as a means of bringing parties to a dispute together, but the realities of power politics were once again becoming the accepted basis of international relations.

In fact, the Labor Government had never doubted this and was only willing to work and fight for the effectiveness of the United Nations as a peacekeeping force on the understanding that the rest of the world showed an equal willingness to accede to the principles on which it had been based and for which it was supposed to stand. Labor's efforts in the United Nations were subsidiary to the mainstream of Australian foreign and defence policy, but this was not the way it always appeared to the Australian electorate.

In some respects the Government was forced by strong Opposition criticism into a position whereby it had to defend its confidence in the United Nations to a further degree than it would have wished, just as the Opposition had earlier been forced to be distortedly critical of the United Nations by virtue of their parliamentary function. By placing the Government in an exaggeratedly false position the Opposition was able to capitalise on the Government's policies in public far more than the facts warranted. A similar position existed over the American alliance, even though Evatt had taken several, little publicised steps towards a formal security arrangement.

The anti-Russo-Communist theme which emerged was fed from both external and internal sources, and this combination proved overpowering in its force. By 1949, it had infiltrated most aspects of party policy in one way or another, and it was inevitable that foreign and defence policy should receive a heavy share of the contamination.

The Opposition had a ready-made issue in the trade union ban on Dutch ships which they had already successfully exploited to a minor extent in the 1946 campaign. Despite the Dutch "police action" of July, 1947, and the air of legitimacy which anti-Dutch sentiment received when the issue was subsequently placed before the Security Council, Government critics were able to maintain a steady pressure by using, with little development, the theme of communist waterfront control of foreign policy.

The Manus Island question, once it had become clear that no agreement was going to be reached over the continuation of an American presence, was also extended from one election to the next and played upon by Opposition speakers who attempted to show that Government policy was eliminating the hope of United States support if the need arose. In a similar way as in the case of the Dutch ships, there was little development of the original argument, except in the context of the increasing urgency due to the world security situation.

A further aspect of the Government's handling of foreign policy which carried over from the 1946 election, was the constant neglect it was afforded in parliamentary debate, and the way in which Evatt continued to monopolise the field. The two were, in fact connected, and this assumed an added significance since, if the Opposition were successful in creating an impression of Evatt failing it would reflect directly and totally on the Government as a whole – and Evatt was becoming increasingly vulnerable. By early 1949, the situation had aroused *The Sydney Morning Herald* enough for it to issue an editorial censure:

The Commonwealth Parliament's neglect of foreign affairs, long notorious, has become scandalous and dangerous in the present tense state of international relations … In the absence of Dr. Evatt, Cabinet never seems to know enough about its – or his – foreign policy to keep Parliament informed.

*

One significant feature of the 1949 campaign which had not been present in 1946 was the issue of defence forces and its offshoot, compulsory military service. The Labor Government had been responsible for the demobilisation and repatriation of the huge wartime armed forces, and, considering the size of the task, this was done smoothly and without undue criticism. The nature of Australia's post-war armed forces remained under review for some months after the war's end while service chiefs and defence ministers worked on plans.

By early 1947, however, vague statements about Australia as being the "arsenal for the Empire", or co-operation with Britain, and closely integrated military services were becoming insufficient to avert increasing criticism of what the *Sydney Morning Herald* in November, 1946, called the Government's "wait and see" policy. Once Chifley had announced a five-year defence plan in June, 1947, criticism shifted to the plan's inadequacy and the lack of progress which was being made, especially in recruiting, as pointedly expressed by General Thomas Blamey at the time. As the plan was being put into effect, it gradually became obvious that the recruiting drive was, in fact, not meeting with success.

In April, 1948, the Minister for Defence, J.J. Dedman, assured Australians that the defence plan progress was "satisfactory". By July, Dedman was promising a "review" of the plan if the system failed. In September he attempted to-redirect defence emphasis by stating that "scientific research" was the "number one defence priority" (perhaps influenced by his responsibility for the CSIRO), but by February, 1949, he was forced to admit that the defence programme was "not proceeding as fast as the Government would like".

This allowed Government critics to add to their attack the need for compulsory military service as the only possible means for adequately filling army requirements. During 1948 and 1949 this attack on defence policy, including the call for compulsory military service, was maintained with a monotonous and relentless persistence and gathered strength as new voices were added to the chorus of disquiet.

These included the Federal Executive of the RSL, Lieutenant-General Morshead and twelve other citizen generals, the annual conference of the Legion of Ex-Servicemen, the Government's own military advisors and General Blamey, and the Commonwealth Council of Defence. What is more telling, criticism did not seem to be confined to non-Labor supporters. The triennial Federal ALP Conference of September, 1948, amended the Party's platform to allow military forces to be sent overseas in time of war, and there were many members of the ALP, including some ex-service members in Parliament, who wanted a speed-up in the defence programme. A few of these, with an eye to the coming elections, even supported the introduction of compulsory military training.

By October, 1949, two months before the elections, the "Canberra Correspondent" of the *Sydney Morning Herald* could confidently predict that "defence will be a big election issue".

One point on which Evatt's, and hence the Government's policy gained fairly widespread support was the occupation of Japan and the negotiations for a Japanese peace treaty. Most sections of Australian society were openly hostile towards Japan and Evatt's efforts to secure an early Peace Conference in the face of increasing United States leniency towards the Japanese met with approval. (An exception was Sydney's Cardinal Norman Gilroy who made a tour of Japan in mid-1949 and stressed the bond that existed between Australia and Japan through the link of Japan's Catholic community, praising the non-warlike nature of the Japanese and their desire for a lasting peace.)

In any case, the diplomatic intricacies and the technical confusions of the occupation made it difficult for much opinion to form articulately, but there was general agreement that the victory against Japan which had been won so dearly should not be lost through inadvertence, and Evatt appeared to be handling the situation in Australia's best interests. This, and the fact that much real interest at the popular level had faded away, explains why the Japanese question was not raised during the campaign.

*

The 1949 campaign was one of the most bitter of the post-war election campaigns. Menzies, leading the Liberal Country Party Opposition, knew that the tide of opinion was running strongly in his favour, and he was intent on tapping it as best he could. The theme he chose, or the theme that was in many ways chosen for him by the Government, was the drift to socialism – the slow eatingaway of Australia's "free enterprise" society.

This attack on "socialisation", as it was called, was hotly pressed by Opposition speakers and supporters throughout the campaign. The Government lost the initiative early in the piece, and was never to regain it. Although the lines along which the Opposition was to pursue the foreign policy debate had been clearly marked out by Menzies before the campaign had even commenced, under the circumstances, foreign affairs was forced to take a back seat as an election issue. It was, on occasions, linked to the socialism theme in passing reference, but rarely was there any detailed exposition or defence of policy by either side.

Considering the advantage the Opposition could have expected to gain from an attack on Evatt, the Government's policy for the United Nations and Indonesia, and the apparent withdrawal of the United States from the South-west Pacific, this may appear strange. The answer lies in the fact that, once again, the major points could be scored off the Government by attacking domestic policies, and hence, any time spent on foreign affairs was relatively wasted. In any event, as Menzies had said: "Foreign affairs would never be electioneering stuff in Australia because it had not a broad public appeal".

Another contributing factor to the lack of debate was the undoubted absence of any disagreement between the parties over the basic assumptions of Australian foreign policy at the time, perhaps due to the relative weakness of its national power, perhaps due to that focus on domestic issues. To be sure, there were wide differences of opinion over methods and specific policy points, but these were often too involved or too technical to be handled with justice on the hustings, especially under the stress of circumstances of 1949.

This state of affairs did not go unrecognised

at the time, and contemporary commentators were always quick to seize upon it as an excuse to explain the neglect of foreign affairs. The Canberra Political Correspondent of The Hobart Mercury, Frank Chamberlain, noted in the early stages of the campaign:

On foreign policy there is very little to choose between the two sides of politics. There is a difference of emphasis, but it is patent that plans now being laid in Canberra for future Australian policy towards Southeast Asia will be largely followed by any change of government.

The Sydney Morning Herald confirmed this opinion when it commented, two days before the poll:

If external affairs have entered but little into the present election campaign, it is because there is no real quarrel between the Government and the Opposition on the basic aims which should activate our foreign policy.

Even the Liberal Party itself, in the form of its Defence Policy Committee, of which General Blamey was now a member, could declare at the beginning of the campaign that it would adopt "four main points of the Government's defence policy: (1) Conclusion of a Pacific Pact with the United States; (2) Development of Australia as a main support area for the British Commonwealth in the Pacific; (3) The joint AngloAustralian defence research project in South Australia; (4) The Snowy Mountains hydro-electric scheme". The only significant difference from Government policy this same Committee, in fact, recommended was the introduction of compulsory military training.

During late 1948 Menzies had made an oversea trip through North America and Britain. On his return, in 1949, he gave a series of addresses in most capital cities, in each of which he outlined the Opposition's foreign policy as it would be put forward later in the year. The significant point which emerged from these addresses was that Menzies, and hence the Opposition, was placing a great deal of confidence in the continuing appeal of British Empire solidarity and the need for British-American unity. Speaking in Perth in January he said:

Australia's international task was to strive for two things: (1) The highest possible degree of unanimity among British peoples so that, as far as possible, they could speak with one voice; (2) Encouragement in every way of Anglo-American understanding and joint action.

At the same time, a fortnight later in Sydney, he was able to connect the domestic anti-socialism theme to foreign policy in two ways. Firstly, he was finally convinced that it was time "the Western democracies made a stand against

Russia", a policy which linked well with the Opposition's domestic criticism of "fifth column Communists". Second, he was able to stigmatize the word "Socialist" even further by associating the British Labour Government, the New Zealand Labour Government, and the Australian Labor Government in the supposed unfortunate developments which had taken place in the British Commonwealth:

In the last six months, Socialist administrations in the British world have been steadily and consciously retreating from what ought to be our greatness. Every conceivable move is made that will diminish the British element and the significance of the Crown in our make-up, and convert us from an ancient powerful family, bound by family ties, into a loose alliance of casually friendly nations.

A totally misrepresentative argument but one which Menzies was using cleverly.

When Menzies came to deliver the Opposition Policy Speech nine months later in the now traditional location of Camberwell in his Kooyong electorate (although he completed it the next day in Melbourne), the ideas he expressed on foreign and defence policy were almost identical to these. The cohesive factor in the speech was the call for greater British Empire co-operation and integration, and for a halt in the tendency brought about by the "Socialists" towards "weakening the organic links of the Crown".

The United Nations did not figure at all in Menzies' thinking, receiving what might be called contemptuous attention:

We are … not to cultivate distant fields, unless such cultivation has a bearing upon our own pastures … In short, our first League of Nations, tried in many fires, is the British Commonwealth and Empire

There was to be close co-ordination of all Australia's defence arrangements with British countries, as well as improved means of consultation so that "in all fateful days we may speak with one voice". Menzies also wanted to see closer economic collaboration to the extent of calling an "immediate Empire Economic Conference". Beyond this emphasis on British Empire affairs ("if the Socialists would still permit the word 'British' to be used", he sniffed), little was contemplated except "close co-operation between the Commonwealth and Empire and the United States of America". Passing reference was made to the need for a "good-neighbour policy in the South-west Pacific," and there was mention of a "prompt, just and lasting peace settlement" with Germany and Japan, and of the necessity to avoid "the control of foreign policy by persons other than Parliament and Government"- a remark clearly aimed at the waterfront unions' ban on Dutch ships.

In relation to the Policy Speech as a whole, however, this outline of foreign and defence policy was extremely brief, and it was obvious that Menzies was granting it little more than obligatory attention. The emphasis was on an attack on the socialist state and its objectives, and on an emotional defence of free private enterprise and "freedom". As *The Sydney Morning Herald* put it, Menzies was asking whether Australia was "to remain predominantly a free-enterprise country or [was] it to follow the path of socialisation marked out for it by the Chifley Government".

Menzies' most significant point as far as the campaign and defence policy was concerned, was his very vague reference to compulsory military training, or "universal military physical training for periods suited to our conditions, and by methods, and on conditions as to call-up and numbers, to be determined by the best expert advice".

Menzies returned to foreign affairs or defence policies only once again during the campaign; in Hobart on November 29, and only then to repeat almost verbatim what he had said in his Kooyong speech about the "Socialists" and Empire, the Commonwealth as the "first and last League of Nations", and the need for close ties between

"British countries" and the United States. This event was such a rare one that it prompted the *Sunday Herald's* "Political Correspondent" to write a few days later:

For the first time during the campaign Mr. Menzies deviated from the line he has set himself, of hammering the socialist theme to the virtual exclusion of lesser issues, to expound the Opposition's foreign policy in some detail.

Needless to say, Menzies' Tasmanian speech was not given any other coverage by the mainland press.

Nor were foreign affairs taken up to any great extent by the Opposition's other main spokesmen, Casey and Spender. Casey devoted the greatest share of his attention, on the few occasions he touched on foreign policy, to the American relationship and the "offhand and slighting treatment that Mr. Chifley's Government" had given the United States. The vacating of Manus Island was "a piece of criminal folly" in Casey's opinion: "My American friends had asked why the Chifley Government had 'kicked' the American forces out of Manus Island."

Casey's ideas of foreign policy, as he expressed them during the campaign, were less narrowly based than those of most other participants in the debate. He looked beyond the immediate needs of security via defence arrangements (though these were automatically included), to foreign aid for the development of the country. This could only be achieved by "close collaboration with Australia's friends, and not by our own efforts alone". In fact, the import of Casey's approach was Australia's need for friends – America and Britain, as well as the countries to the north – and his attack lay in his claim that Evatt and Chifley were pursuing the type of policy which discouraged close relationships: "Trying to 'outsmart' the other fellow may bring an immediate dividend, but does not encourage or promote long-term friendship and confidence".

The exception to these passing references was a full article by Casey published in The Argus, Melbourne, on November 25, "Australia's Relations with the World", which set out his ideas in some detail. As was Hughes' newspaper article for the 1946 campaign, this article was the most intensive elaboration of the Opposition's case published during the 1949 campaign. It would suggest that these matters were best reserved for the written explication rather than tossed around willy-nilly at potentially rowdy gatherings.

Once again Casey referred to Australia's relative weakness due to its small population (around 8 million) and the need to work with the "great co-operative society, the British Race, of which the senior partner is our Mother Country,

Mud Map to AUKUS

Great Britain". Though not to diminish "the very great potential asset of the friendship of the greatest single nation in the world, the United States of America. Geographically, we are the most important outpost of European settlement on our side of the world". It was cringeworthy material by today's standards and in today's environment, but equally, with a substitution of terms, it could easily be applied to more recent strategic arrangements such as AUKUS. The article continued in these terms, repeating his line on the need to increase our population and for national development within the power structure of those two Great Powers, to increase our defence spending in line with Britain and the US, as well as attacking Labor over Manus Island. He ended with a brief call for Australia to make "friends" to the North, which stretched as far as the Middle East, but once again it was based on the need for Australia to remain British rather than integrate with Asia.

Spender did not concentrate on foreign affairs at all, and, in any case, his views on foreign policy had not altered much from those he expressed in 1946. The target of his attack was still Evatt's international bias, in contrast to an Australian bias as it should have been. Evatt was still the man of book learning who did not yet understand "that logic does not settle the affairs of men, does not often, if at all, help Australia, though no doubt it does afford to himself the means of world notoriety". This, in more recent times, would no doubt be referred to as the "tall-poppy syndrome'. Australian foreign policy, to Spender, was still negligent in respect to Australia's "vital interests to the north", due in part to Evatt's involvement with United Nations problems" in Palestine and all points west". But even Spender was too concerned with domestic issues to develop his attack any further than this. Other Liberals were similarly occupied, preferring to follow the lines set down by Menzies in his policy speech, especially on Empire co-operation, than to make any outstanding contribution of their own. O.H. Beale, Member for Parramatta, for example, could only manage the following, despite later becoming a senior diplomat as ambassador to the US: "The Liberals believed in the British Empire because it was a League of Nations that really worked."

The only Opposition spokesman who appears to have injected a novel note into an otherwise dull, straightforward and scanty foreign affairs debate was the Country Party leader, Fadden. During a tour of Queensland in the last few campaign days, perhaps influenced by his location and the heightened awareness there of any threat from the North, in Brisbane on December 8, he warned

Australians against being caught unawares by the "Red tide from South-east Asia". He also made a rare reference to the recent communist victory in China. Rumours were rife during the election campaign about the Government's intentions regarding recognition of Communist China. In no way, however, was either party willing to be drawn out into committing itself in debate.

Fadden was the most vehement of the Opposition's anti-communist group, and it was not an unexpected line of attack for him to connect external affairs with domestic issues:

Mr. Chifley and his ministers are blind to the fact that a major war is already raging on the battlefronts of China, where Communist forces are thrusting their Red spearpoints towards Australia. They are blind to the fact that advance guards of Communist forces have been extremely active in the pattern of guerrilla war through Burma, Siam, Malaysia, and Indonesia, which has already resulted in the cold-blooded murder of Englishmen and Australians. Nobody can deny a similar fifth column is operating in Australia as part of a conspiracy for world conquest, sabotage of our industries and defence activities.

He was apparently referring to the killing, probably by communist guerrillas, of several English and Australian workers at outlying plantation in Malaya. The Opposition campaign also included posters depicting an arrow, representing Chinese Communism, aimed at the heart of Australia. Fadden's outburst was in fact an early and fairly isolated foretaste of an issue which was to feature far more seriously in future federal election campaigns.

Another actor on the political scene as vehemently anti-communist as Fadden was J.T. Lang, the former N.S.W. Premier. He had formed an alternative Labor Party of his own and had run for the House of Representatives successfully in 1946 in the Reid electorate on Liberal Party preferences. He proved to be a ferocious opponent of the Labor Government, and Chifley in particular, and was always an impressive parliamentary performer. He switched to the new seat of Blaxland (later held for almost 30 years by Paul Keating) and lost badly, leaving Reid (later held by Tom Uren for over 30 years) to a colleague who also lost badly. He was also highly critical of A.A. Calwell, Immigration Minister, for his regular deportation of Asians (as often various editorials were also, despite any hypocrisy involved), connecting this to his anti-communist foreign policy stance, while somehow reconciling it with his support for White Australia.

Lang delivered his (own) Party's policy speech on November 16, linking this with a potential US alliance and some vague Asian strategic arrangement, calling for "a pact of mutual assistance with the US" and asserting that "Australia would not get [such a pact] while the Government alienated America's potential allies in the Pacific". It was somewhat of a sideshow, ignored by most, but even by its wayward nature showing how foreign affairs had become almost an irrelevance in the public debate.

*

The Government's coverage of foreign affairs was as dismal as their opponents' efforts, mainly due to the fact that they were fully engaged defending their domestic policies. Chifley's policy speech of 14 November which, as Menzies' had been, was delivered in two parts. The first part was broadcast by Chifley from Canberra, and the second was in the form of a supplement issued concurrently. Both parts were published in the metropolitan morning press. It merely brushed on foreign policy, giving purely formal recognition to the United Nations. The Government, Chifley said, had

... given its full support to the United Nations through which it has made an outstanding contribution towards ensuring the effectiveness of international machinery to maintain world peace, order, security, and improved economic conditions.

No more the proud enunciation of the United

Nations' achievements and its future prospects, or of the place of the United Nations in Australia's security arrangements. Instead, Labor, too, turned its full attention towards British Commonwealth defence co-operation and integrated defence arrangements, no doubt to a great extent in response to popular reception of the Opposition's similar appeal. There was indeed, very little to choose now between the co-ordination of British Commonwealth defences which the Opposition proposed, and that which the Government was both putting into effect and publicising:

The defence programme is essentially based on co-operation in British Commonwealth defence. Britain is the heart of the British Commonwealth. It is vital to our security and our economy that we continue to co-operate with the United Kingdom. Planning is actively proceeding between (sic) Britain, Australia, and New Zealand on mutual defence.

Any difference that existed, at least in the public broadcasting of the parties' policies, was slight and hinged on the Government's conception of Australia as a supplier of material resources rather than manpower – this itself was more a rebuttal of the Opposition's conscription platform than a policy:

The form of the defence effort was resolved by those things which Australia could do best to co-operate in

Mud Map to AUKUS

British Commonwealth defence.

It is a wonder whether it was worth saying. The foreign policy debate had certainly reached its nadir.

The Minister for External Affairs, Evatt, himself made only one significant incursion into the field of foreign affairs during the campaign period. This neglect in itself is an indication of how far Evatt and his policies had lost the favourable following which they had commanded three years previously – and of how far Evatt and the Labor Party had lost confidence in their own policies as vote-catchers. Evatt's personal vote in the Barton electorate, for instance, fell sharply, from about 67% to 53% preferred. It would be too simple to say that this was due to any one factor, since there had been a redistribution of the Barton boundaries and his new opponent was Nancy Wake, the war hero of french resistance fame, but certainly his standing as an international figure was not strong enough by itself to hold his vote any longer.

Evatt's statement, in the *Sydney Morning Herald* of December 8, was a direct reply to Casey's article published two weeks earlier, and it showed little development in Evatt's basic policy points. There was still a determination to place confidence in the United Nations as a means of solving international disputes "upon the basis not of mere power or mere expediency, but of right and of justice", though he himself was now at times acting on the basis of expediency. Evatt followed his leader's pattern of a declaration of British Commonwealth co-operation and close friendship with America.

What differences were there now between the two sides' public declarations? One explanation is that they no longer, for the time being at least, cared. In an obvious attempt to counteract Casey's criticism of the Government's handling of relationships with the United States Evatt repeated the Government's policy of reciprocity in the use of bases; as far as the public was concerned there had been no development in this policy since 1946 – in 1946 it was controversial, if impractical, in 1949 it was simply irrelevant. Evatt went on to admit implicitly that negotiations for a Pacific Pact with the United States had reached a deadlock, adding at the same time a covering explanation:

Broadly speaking, both the Australian and American Governments have agreed that the relationships between their two countries were and are so close and intimate that a formal regional pact of the kind envisaged was not required.

This rather startling claim – or admission – evoked no reply, no probing questioning, despite the fact that a Pacific Pact with the United States was a Liberal Party plank of some importance. The election was a mere two days away, and attention was drawn to more urgent and momentous matters.

During the early part of the campaign an undercurrent of discussion on compulsory military training served as a prop for the arguments over defence policy. Both Chifley, in Brisbane on November 17, and Calwell, in Parkside on November 25, had strongly denied during speeches that conscription, under the circumstances existing, was required. Calwell relied on an argument straight from the Labor platform, that conscription was unjustified "except in the case of the imminence of war or the danger of an attack on Australia", and Chifley claimed that there were "much more valuable things" to be done for the defence of Australia. By late November, they had been joined by Evatt who added that conscription would be a drain on industrial manpower and would eventually prove harmful to Australia's defence potential.

One metropolitan daily newspaper, *The Argus* (Melbourne*)*, by this time decided in an editorial that "defence was an issue", and so, it seems, did the Labor Party, since the conscription issue suddenly gained much attention from Government speakers. Labor campaign organisers began inserting advertisements with primary attention being drawn to the disruptive effect of "Menzies' compulsory call-ups". Dedman became the fourth Minister to treat conscription as an important issue, using Evatt's original argument that industrial development would be impaired. By December 5, Menzies felt it was time to refute the over-exaggerations of some of the Government's supporters' statements about numbers and methods of call-up, as well as such statements as Calwell made about "Australian children being conscripted into military service" by the Liberals, but was suitably vague. He made no effort to justify by argument the necessity of introducing such a drastic step:

We have far too much sense to denude industry of manpower. The number to be called up and trained, having regard to our resources, is extremely limited, We shall in due course introduce a scheme suitable to our resources.

By December 7, *The Argus* in an editorial confidently believed that conscription was "the vital issue", and both leaders had given their most elaborate statements of their respective cases, Chifley on December 6 in Hurstville, Sydney, and Menzies in his final election broadcast the next day. Chifley believed any withdrawal of labour from the workforce would be highly detrimental to the nation, especially since a large immigration programme was underway to counteract this very danger. On top of this, the need for conscription was not apparent: "There is no danger of war", was Chifley's final word on the subject.

Menzies' case, on the other hand, was based on the uncertain and dangerous nature of the international situation and the fact that other Western nations had undertaken forms of military training:

Can we gamble on the chance, which we have had before, of an interval of months before the first battle? Surely our best guarantee of peace is that … we shall make such earnest preparations for the defence of liberty.

Conscription, almost certainly, was not a "vital issue" in the 1949 elections. Opinion polls taken regularly from 1943 through to 1950 showed the Australian electorate was consistently and clearly in favour in a ratio of about 4 to 1 of some form of military conscription, only slightly less in peacetime, and with only minor variation across the political spectrum. The issue was more an attempt by Labor to make a stand on a point they felt could gain some sympathy and on which some felt very strongly, in the face of an interminable barrage from the Opposition on domestic anti-socialism propaganda which was having an obviously corrosive effect on Labor' support. Whether or not it decided significant numbers of votes will never be resolved, but it provides an interesting example of how, in a limited way, points of policy can be drawn out from both sides by intense debate and proper publicity. It also shows how election campaigns, even on such a polemical issue as conscription, fail to provide an adequate means by which well reasoned and well-balanced cases can be presented for popular decision.

*

The 1949 election campaign proved the extent to which foreign and defence policies could be pushed into the background by the pressure of urgent domestic matters. It also showed how, when such policies were treated thus, they became ragged and indistinct. The differences between the parties' policies were certainly not apparent, but the seeds of conflict were underneath the surface waiting to germinate. Australian policies found themselves in a rather confused state of affairs in the midst of transition into a new era.

The Labor Party was still shaking itself free of the image it had saddled itself with in respect to the United Nations; the Opposition could not for much longer speak as it did in terms of "Empire" co-operation. The Opposition assumed that the world was still governed by force and its policies matched this assumption: conscription, stronger defence, security arrangements with more powerful allies –

these policies were more in tune with an electorate which looked upon the worsening "cold war" confrontation with a growing dismay and fear and could no longer find comfort in the claims which Labor had made about the United Nations. Labor was not unaware of the facts of the world situation, but it was caught up by its own past assertions and it was too slow to sort its new policies out.

On December 10, 1949, almost five million Australians went to the polls to elect a Liberal Country Party Government, thus beginning a succession of electoral defeats for the ALP With the Liberal Country Party victory came a distinct new period in Australian foreign policy. It was the end of a period, unique in Australian political history, when Labor ideas on foreign relations dominated the Australian political scene and commanded, for a while, widespread popularity with the electorate.

CONCLUSION

ELECTION campaigns were, and are, highly unsuitable for the successful discussion of foreign affairs. Even during such a period as 1943-1949, when foreign affairs received an unusual amount of attention on a national scale, the impact of policy during the election period was negligible. The exception to this was in 1946 when Evatt's popular image was a noted electoral advantage for the ALP, although even here the influence of foreign policy was indirect. It was Evatt's image, the idea the public had of Evatt's work overseas, which impressed Australian voters, rather than the various aspects of policy which he was pursuing.

The explanation for this failure on the part of foreign policy to make a direct impression lies in a number of factors, some of which are general, some of which are peculiar to the period. There is no doubt that as a popular issue foreign affairs had no appeal (defence policy in simplified forms, such as conscription, could raise a certain amount of heated partisanship). The electorate, while not totally apathetic, was not concerned with nice debate over the United Nations, the British Commonwealth or the United States relationship. Hence, Menzies would use emotional appeals to "family ties" to arouse disquiet about Evatt's occasional disagreement with British policy, while

Evatt would talk about "international peace based on justice" in an effort to gain sympathy for his United Nations policy and his counter criticisms about "power politics".

Although there were several attempts to connect foreign policy to domestic issues, the ban on Dutch ships being the notable example, domestic considerations dominated political attitudes, and more so as the country resumed "business as usual". Even in the case of the Dutch ships it is significant that the domestic factors soon came to outweigh any advantage or disadvantage which had accrued over the international aspects.

Foreign and defence policy always had reserved to it a distinct portion of the parties' policy speeches, but this could mean that the foreign policy as delivered during policy speeches was a very scant and worthless summary of very general assumptions. The same could be applied to the campaigns as a whole, especially with Chifley's and Menzies' speeches in 1949.

By and large, debate during the hectic campaign weeks was complicated by the obvious lack of differences in basic party policies. Differences there were, but they were too complex or obscure to warrant careful, analytical and time consuming attention during a period when schedules were at their tightest.

Yet it is too simple to say that the reason for this lack of divisive issues lay in Australia's insufficient national power, or in a concentration on domestic problems, for Australians were always willing to divide over matters, even external ones, if indeed they disagreed, such as on Indonesia (and later, of course, over Vietnam). Similarly, concentration on domestic matters did not detract from discussion of foreign affairs totally, but in many ways took place because there was little interest in foreign affairs. Once an issue was raised, whether foreign policy or defence policy, there was no inadequacy of argument. Witness the last-minute flurry over conscription in 1949. The true reason lies in the fact that Australian national attitudes were too similar, and it was reflected in party policy. People wanted close ties with America; they were fond of British ties, were unhappy to see them changing, but accepted it; they wished to live in friendship with Asian nations and help them to develop and without foreign (especially Japanese) military interference but were equally anxious about any threat that may come from the north; they hoped the United Nations would prove successful, but weren't optimistic. With such common national basic assumptions there was little room left for disagreement.

Neither Government nor Opposition could launch large-scale, that is, vote-winning, attacks on the other, either because the policies were too popular, or they were too similar. Campaign statements thus tended to become very vague and general summaries which attempted to put a highly involved set of principles and factors into easily understandable form. The nature of campaigning precluded any detailed worthwhile analysis of foreign policy issues. Hence no debate originated on the problem of Japan's future role in the Pacific, or the nature of the informal American alliance, while at the same time there was an abundance of catchwords, slogans and cant phrases about the British Commonwealth and Empire, countries to the north, international peace and security, and the communist menace.

Apart from these negative aspects of foreign and defence policy electioneering, the part which the three campaigns played in the development of policy, or in the development of public attitudes to policy, was also insubstantial. Because the statements of participants were as stereotyped and generalised as they were, campaigns, at best, tended to reinforce attitudes rather than change them.

Above all, election campaigns are the precinct of politicians, and politics dominates them in consequence. The politicians are searching for votes, hence what they say is judged to be what the electorate would like to hear. Very few risks are taken. The one exception, and in reality still a very non-adventurous exception, was Curtin's digression on British Imperial relations. Here was an example of a campaign speech receiving such favourable reaction that it prompted further development soon after the elections. Curtin was perhaps testing public reaction to a line of policy in this case, but it was the only example of such thinking. Evatt, in 1943, was rather preparing and shaping public attitudes over an international organisation to his own liking and due to his confidence in it, than testing reaction to such a step.

Overall, the period saw a gradual deterioration, after a brisk and optimstic start, in international affairs, in the consistency and logic of Australian policies, and in the public broadcasting of those policies. The election campaigns reflect this. The enthusiasm which was apparent in the late war years and the early post-war period, and which was due to the idealism naturally existing after the sufferings of war, victory, and the prospects of an entirely different type of peace, gradually receded.

The growing realisation that the international situation had again become critical and power-based (if indeed, it were ever different) was also reflected in the nature of the campaigns. The vague but hopeful statements of 1943, and the more definite though still idealistic viewpoints of 1946, by 1949 had given way to a heavy concentration on security arrangements based on military matters.

Policies, as they were being pursued by the Government, were given a relatively representative airing, though the occasions were rare when specific points of policy with a high controversy potential received attention. Evatt's late admission of the failure of the Pacific Pact planning was one exception; the Japanese Peace Treaty and recognition of Communist China are two examples which received no mention.

The breadth of policy which was covered during the campaigns was typical, in a limited way, of that discussed during the interelection years. The debate produced by the campaigns, however, failed to elucidate or improve the public awareness of issues, though for a short period it probably succeeded in raising a very general interest in some aspects. The final intense volleys over conscription in 1949 may be cited as an exception, but even these did not produce a detailed and rational case either for or against the issue, nor did they change viewpoints to any significant degree.

Nevertheless, the parties and the participants were always sensitive to reactions to their statements of policy from both the public and their opponents. They were at times prepared to highlight a certain factor which was drawing favourable responses or to take up a variation of the other side's policy if it was proving popular. Evatt's personal popularity and the importance of British Commonwealth co-operation in 1946 are examples. Parties were likewise always ready to play down a point if it was clearly proving a handicap to their campaigning, as Menzies did with the entire field of foreign affairs in 1946, or, alternatively to grant it scant attention if it was irrelevant to the outcome of the elections, as both parties did in 1949.

With minor exceptions, where foreign and defence policy is concerned, election campaigns have an extremely superficial and somewhat formal part to play. The dictates of politics are too powerful for a reasonable and far-sighted approach to prevail.

This is no less the case now than it was then. When Australia's involvement in the Korean War and the Malayan "Emergency" in the 1950s then "Konfrontasi" brought foreign affairs and defence to the fore in the form of actual conflict once again, and even when foreign affairs took dramatic centre stage during the Vietnam War years, far more heat than light on the subject was generated during the election campaigns of the period. And when it came to military interventions of more recent times such as in the Gulf War, Iraq and Afghanistan (included in Casey's definition in 1949 of our sphere of engagement), or with the signing of the ANZUS Treaty in 1951, the same political and social forces have been at play: little disagreement in the substance of policies across most of the political spectrum, and little public interest in the issues being debated in general.

A similar lack of public awareness, let alone discussion, exists of the "Five Eyes" security arrangement – who has even heard of the UKUSA Agreement, its official title? – or The Quadrilateral Security Dialogue, known as "The Quad", a dialogue definitely denied to close public scrutiny. There is also AUSMIN, the vehicle for direct consultations between Australia and the United States at ministerial level. What is even more starkly revealing is the lead-up and inauguration by announcement of the AUKUS security agreement of 2021. In this case there was nil preparation through debate or discussion, and to all intents and purposes nil or at most muted dissent immediately afterwards, There were some early murmurs from the ALP concerning Australia's potential loss of independence or sovereignty, with which Curtin would have undoubtedly concurred, but generally strategic outlook and policies of the two major parties have become bipartisan.

Mud Map to AUKUS

Boris Johnson, for his part, referred to the "raucous squawkers of the anti-AUKUS caucus", possibly aimed at the French as much as anywhere. Once more time for consideration had passed, some analysts and commentators, such as Andrew Podger of the ANU, Hans-J. Ohff of the University of Adelaide (who also pointed out the lack of involvement of both the public and the parliament in the decision), Peter Jennings of the Australian Strategic Policy Institute and Greg Sheridan in The Australian, began casting doubts on the details, but much of it turned on the practicalities, or impracticalities, of the submarine programme itself. The Greens, with around 10% mostly young support, eventually grabbed the opportunity of clear differentiation by denouncing the arrangement (and by doing so tacitly acknowledging the Chinese military threat), calling for a renegotiation of the American alliance and a policy of demilitarisation along the New Zealand model. Former Prime Minister Paul Keating also weighed in, characteristically with a completely contrarian argument that attempting to contain China with "matchstick" submarines was a mug's game. If nothing else, debate, and disparate views, over foreign and defence policy had now firmly established itself in the modern Australian political vernacular.

Mud Map to AUKUS

Nevertheless, as before, mainstream consensus (having been presented with a fait accompli) amongst the electorate continued on the cause and need – a threat from the North. An opinion poll taken soon after the announcement found voters 2 to 1 in support of the arrangement but 5 to 1 that the danger came from the North, i.e. China. (It is intriguing to speculate where the minority thought it may come from – perhaps New Zealand and the Pacific island nations could turn nasty under Chinese influence or hegemony; would Chinese military bases in Antarctica still constitute a threat from the North?)

It would seem, then, that the pillars of Australia's foreign policy that had been enunciated ad infinitum for over 70 years: the British and Commonwealth/Empire/anglosphere heritage and ties (though now with the notable absence of New Zealand), squeezing out the French, now neatly allowing for India to be gradually engaged in the mechanism and so introducing a not purely semantic terminological change from "Asia-Pacific" to "Indo-Pacific"; the US alliance with its security umbrella (our "great and powerful friends"); a threat from somewhere in Asia (the North); the core beliefs and brotherhood of liberal democracies; and lip-service to an organised system for international justice.

And surely it will be "forever" so.

APPENDIX

Political cartoons of the period were very unsubtle in their method of criticism. If the cartoonist assumed a particular position in his comment it was almost inevitably anti-Labor, as the following examples indicate. Graphic comment on foreign policy was not abundant, and the four examples which are reproduced here for 1946 and the two for 1949 were the only relevant ones contained in the newspapers consulted for these two campaign periods. There was little cartoon commentary on relevant issues during the war or during the wartime election campaign. The other four cartoons are a selection of the more pertinent ones from the inter-election period.

The four ALP advertisements speak for themselves and, in any case, are related to the text. In three of the examples there is probably a superior exposition of policy than appeared most elsewhere during the entire campaigns, with exceptions. It is notable that, just as there were no anti-Opposition cartoons, there were no Opposition advertisements in support of the Opposition's foreign and defence policy, except for one very minor exception of the former which linked the communist-dominated waterfront unions with the dictation of Australia's foreign policy.

Cartoon by Frith, the Sydney Morning Herald, *August 17, 1946, p. 2.*
An early example of the type of attacks that were launched on Evatt's style
in oversea councils.

Mud Map to AUKUS

Mr. Chifley: "Not now, Bert, some other time. We've got to concentrate on this game for a while."

Cartoon by Frith, the Sydney Morning Herald, *August 30, 1946, p. 2. Another example of the impression many Australians received of Evatt's handling of his portfolio. (Note the contrast between Frith's depiction of the apparently affectionate relationship between Evatt and Molotov and that of Molnar on the page following.)*

STATE OF THE NATION . . . By Molnar

Cartoon by Molnar, the Daily Telegraph, *August 31, 1946, p. 11. A typical critical attitude of Evatt's policy both abroad, in its aggressive pretentiousness, and at home, in its bowing to the dictation of "undemocratic" influences.*

EVATT

must carry on!

"I know of no modern statesman who has been more constructive and more courageous in the fight for the establishment of a prac-tical and realistic basis of democratic principles than **Dr. Evatt.**"

H. SUMNER WELLS. 11.8.48.

Dr. H. V. Evatt, Labor's envoy in the field of international affairs, a man whose courage and ability have been hailed throughout the world, whose work has given Australia a higher status than was ever before enjoyed, would become a "back number" if Menzies were returned to power. Menzies would throw him into the political discard.

Yet this is the man who has emblazoned the name "Australia" on the hearts of every nation, who has made Australia the champion of all small nations, who has fought domination and tyranny tooth and nail.

This is the man who battles for overseas markets for Australian goods and produce, who has given Australia a solid and constructive foreign policy, and made Australia's Labor Government respected wherever thinking people congregate.

AUSTRALIA cannot afford to withdraw EVATT from the International field

Neither Menzies nor Fadden can offer his equal . . . yet their loyalty to the people is not sufficient to make them admit it

VOTE LABOR

and Return the **CHIFLEY GOVERNMENT**

AND FOR THE SENATE: ☐1 Ashley, W. P.   ☐2 Arnold, J. J.   ☐3 Large, W. J.

Number every square otherwise your vote will be Informal

Authorised by W. E. Dickson, M.L.C., Parliament House, Sydney.

Advertisement inserted on behalf of the ALP in the Daily Telegraph, *September 13, 1946, p. 15.*

As the campaign progressed it became obvious that Evatt's personal standing with the electorate was a powerful electoral advantage in itself, and the ALP capitalised on it. This is an example of the type of appeal that was used.

Cartoon by Molnar, the Daily Telegraph, *September 19, 1946, p. 2. Another example of the criticism levelled at the Government over their handling of the waterfront ban on Dutch shipping.*

[ADVERTISEMENT]

The Gravest Responsibility of All

By DR. H. V. EVATT

"Amidst all the clamour of the election campaign, the ears of the electors have been deafened to one very grave consideration. It is this:—

Unless we are able to prevent a third World War, all plans for tax reductions, for housing, for industrial expansion and productive employment will be mere scraps of paper swept away in an atomic cyclone of death and disaster.

Australia's Labor Government has faced this fact with deep seriousness. It is the fundamental basis of Labor's foreign policy that this country must never again be threatened with invasion and enslavement. Labor realises, however, that the world cannot be "talked" into peace. War cannot be prevented by mere oratory. There must be constructive action.

The root causes of war are economic insecurity of the people and social injustices. Labor's foreign policy is, therefore, directed towards the promotion of economic security, full employment and social justice for all nations. On the successful achievement of these objectives depend Australia's prosperity, security and safety. In other words, every domestic issue raised in the present election campaign depends, in the final analysis, upon the continued implementation of Labor's foreign policy, a policy which has won for Australia the respect and confidence of all nations.

Labor looks upon the assurance of peace, with economic security and full employment, as the gravest responsibility of all. Labor will honour that responsibility."

H. V. EVATT.

POINTS TO REMEMBER ON POLLING DAY

● *Menzies' taxation proposals mean an average reduction of 1/6½ a week to the man earning £8 or less. But they mean, at the same time, a levy of 6/9 a week for social services, if not more.*

● *Menzies' Child Endowment proposal would result in a lower basic wage.*

● *The present disastrous position in America has resulted from abandonment of the very principles applied by Labor Governments in Australia during the last 5 years.*

● *Labor is the ONLY Party pledged to Full Employment, wisely controlled prices and REAL tax reductions.*

Authorised by W. E. Gietzen, Parliament House, Sydney.

TONIGHT: 8.30 to 9 p.m., J. B. Chifley over 2FC and National Relay Stations

Advertisement inserted on behalf of the ALP in the Sydney Morning Herald, *September 25, 1946, p. This is another example of the use of Evatt's image as a vote-catching device.*

THE VOICE OF AUSTRALIA

Mr. Norman Corwin, visiting American radio dramatist, intends to interview as many people as possible in 10 days in an endeavour to gain an accurate impression of Australian thought.

Cartoon by Frith, the Sydney Morning Herald, *September 25, 1946, p. 2. An interesting point to keep in mind, though not directly concerned with foreign and defence policy, was that Australian opinion was a conglomeration of diverse attitudes, as recognised by this contemporary observer. Under the circumstances, then, it is interesting that attitudes towards foreign and defence policy were as non-divisive as they were. Note that Calwell was now regularly depicted as a cockatoo, partly because of his repetitive attacks on the press, and Ward was seen as a very disagreeable and irritating little dog.*

QUICK CHANGE ARTIST

Dr. Evatt, President of UNO, is now attending the Dominion Prime Ministers' Conference in London. Later he will plead the Federal Government's banking case before the Privy Council.

Call Boy: "*You're on for the Prime Ministers' act, sir.*"

Cartoon by Frith, the Sydney Morning Herald, *October 12, 1948, p. 2.*

PENNY A PEEP

The Prime Minister, Mr. Chifley, promised Parliament an opportunity—but not an unrestricted one—to debate foreign affairs.

ATTENDANT: "Have a look if you like, mate, but I don't know if you'll see much."

Cartoon by Frith, the Sydney Morning Herald, *December 4, 1948, p. 2. Criticism was aimed primarily at the lack of parliamentary debate on foreign policy in this cartoon. Evatt tended either to deliver a Ministerial statement or table a report with no ensuing discussion.*

BABES IN THE WOOD

Cartoon by Eyre Jr., the Sydney Morning Herald, *January 10, 1949, p. 2.*
By this time there was growing confusion over the direction in which
Australia's, especially Evatt's, foreign policy was travelling.

Mud Map to AUKUS

THE ESCAPIST

Mr. Menzies, criticising Dr. Evatt's championing of UNO, said it was fantastic to bandy words about fine theories and airy schemes when lawless and revolutionary forces were on the march.

Cartoon be Frith, February 17, 1949, the Sydney Morning Herald, *p. 2. Evatt's involvement with the United Nations was no longer the advantage it once was in the public eye.*

Mud Map to AUKUS

Cartoon by Armstrong, The Argus, November 28, 1949, p. 2. This followed the publication in both The Argus *and the* Sydney Morning Herald, *of a full article on foreign policy by Casey and requires no further explanation.*

AWAITING INSTRUCTIONS

NEWS ITEM: The Waterside Workers' Federation will consult other unions with a view to
lifting the ban on shipping to the Netherlands East Indies.

Cartoon by Frith, the Sydney Morning Herald, *November 30, 1949, p. 2.
The "dictation" of foreign policy by the waterfront unions remained a
similar point of criticism in the 1949 campaign as it was in 1946. There was
little development in the nature of this criticism but it remained a thorn
in the side of the Government. (The portrait on the wall depicting Chifley
as Lincoln was an allusion to several unfortunate comparisons made by
Ministers during the campaign connecting the two men.)*

(ADVERTISEMENT)

LABOR'S DEFENCE POLICY

● Provides £295,000,000 over five years. The first time Australia has had a planned programme over a definite period.

● Places emphasis on this modern age. The long-range weapon project; the Snowy River electric power scheme; and Professor Oliphant's nuclear research programme are examples.

● Keeps men working on farms and in factories.

COMPULSORY "CALL-UPS" UNDER MENZIES

● Would take hundreds of thousands of husbands, sons and sweethearts and put them into uniform for six months.

● Would disrupt production seriously and impair Australia's part in British Commonwealth defence as the supply base of the Pacific.

● Would take away military establishments at present housing migrants who have been brought here to make Australia safe.

AUSTRALIA NEEDS PRODUCTION
NOT MILITARY CONSCRIPTION UNDER MENZIES

═══ For a SAFE Australia ═══

Vote LABOR

Advertisement inserted on behalf of the A.L.P, in the Sunday Herald, *December 4, 1949, p. 11. This advertisement, and the one on the page following, are two examples of the last-minute emphasis which Labor decided to give to the conscription issue. This advertisement sums up the Labor case far better than any statements of speakers during the debate. The advertisement on the next page resorted more to the emotional appeal.*

Advertisement inserted on behalf of the ALP in The Argus, *December 8, 1949, p. 4. See also preceding page.*

IF YOU CAN IMAGINE IT—
"Eddie's in and Curtin's home and dry."

Churchill and Roosevelt receive news of the results of the Australian 1943 election; Eddie being E.J. Ward, member for East Sydney in the House of Representatives for more than 30 years, and "bête noire" of various Prime Ministers. It purports to depict the disdain the Great Powers had towards lesser players in the war. Roosevelt: "Eddie's in and Curtin's home and dry." *If You Can Imagine It, cartoon by Ted Scorfield, The Bulletin, 25 August, 1943.*

Mud Map to AUKUS

BIBLIOGRAPHY

PRIMARY SOURCES:

Newspapers:

The Sydney Morning Herald was generally consulted for the period July, 1943 to December, 1949, inclusive.

The following newspapers were closely consulted for the three campaign and election periods, July – August, 1943; August September, 1946; November – December, 1949, inclusive:

The Sydney Morning Herald; *The Daily Telegraph* (Sydney);
The Argus (Melbourne);
The Mercury (Hobart);
The Australian Worker (weekly)

The West Australian (Perth) (not consulted for 1943 period);

The Sunday Herald (Sydney) (supplementary to *Sydney Morning Herald* for 1949).

Official Publications:

Commonwealth Parliamentary Debates (Both Houses) were consulted where necessary for period June, 1943 to October,1949.

Political Publications:

"Leaflets and Pamphlets for 1946 Elections ", (Mitchell Library, Sydney).

Australian Labor Party, "Labor Speakers' Notes: Federal Referendum and election, 1946", (Mitchell Library, Sydney).

Liberal Party of Australia, "The Case Against Socialist Labour": Background Notes for Candidates, Speakers and Canvassers ", Sydney, Liberal Party Federal Secretariat, 1949. (Mitchell Library, Sydney).

Gallup Polls:

Australian Public Opinion Polls, Numbers 132-755 (July, 1943 to March, 1951), Melbourne (Mitchell Library, Sydney).

Articles:

Eggleston, Sir Frederic, "The U.N. Charter Critically Considered", The Australian Outlook, Vol. I, No. 1 (March, 1947: Vol. I, No. 2 (June, 1947), Vol. I, No. 3 (September, 1947).

Greenwood, Gordon, "Australia's Foreign Policy", The Australian Outlook, Vol. I, No. 1 (March, 1947).

Packer, Gerald, "Defence in Transition", The Australian Outlook, Vol. I, No. 1 (March, 1947).

Phillips, P.D., "War Trends in Australian Opinions", Australia and the Pacific, Australian Institute of Pacific Relations, (Princeton University Press, 1943).

Ross, Lloyd, "Some Factors in the Development of Labour's Foreign Policies", The Australian Outlook, Vol. III, No. 1 (March, 1949).

Ward, J.M., "A New Constitution for Japan", The Australian Outlook, Vol. I, No. 3 (September, 1947).

Mud Map to AUKUS

Books and Pamphlets:

Ball, W. MacMahon, *Japan, Enemy or Ally* (Melbourne, Cassell, 1948).

Evatt, H.V., *Foreign Policy of Australia, Selected Speeches*, November, 1941 to February, 1945, with an introduction by W. MacMahon Ball (Sydney, Angus and Robertson, 1945).

Evatt, H.V., *Australia in World Affairs, Selected Speeches*, March, 1945 to May, 1946, with a foreword by Sir Frederic Eggleston (Sydney, Angus and Robertson, 1946)

Evatt, H.V., *The United Nations* (Melbourne, Oxford University Press, 1948).

Evatt, H.V., *The Task of Nations* (New York, Duell, Sloan and Pearce, 1949).

Evatt, H.V., "Foreword" to Gilmore, R.A., and Warner, D. (eds.), *Near North: Australia and a Thousand Million Neighbours* (Sydney, Angus and Robertson, 1948).

Fairfax, Warwick, ed., *Men, Parties and Politics* (Sydney, John Fairfax, 1943). Reprint of articles and editorials from *The Sydney Morning Herald* published during the 1943 election campaign with an introduction by Warwick Fairfax.

Gilmore, R.A., and Warner, D., eds., *Near North: Australia and a Thousand Million Neighbours* (Sydney, Angus and Robertson, 1948):

Hasluck, Paul, *Workshop of Security* (Melbourne, F.W. Cheshire 1948).

Spender, P.C., *Australia's Foreign Policy: The Next Phase* (Sydney, Privately Printed, 1944). (Mitchell Library, Sydney.)

SECONDARY SOURCES:
Articles:

Duncan, W.G.K., ed., "Australia's Foreign Policy: 1938", 1938 Summer School of the Australian Institute of Political Science.

Hasluck, Paul, "Australia and the Formation of the United Nations", Royal Australian Historical Society, Journal and Proceedings, Vol. XL, Part III (1954) pp. 133-178.

Books:

Albinski, Henry S., *Australia's Policies and Attitudes Towards China* (Princeton University Press, 1965).

Burton, John W., *The Alternative* (Sydney, Morgans Publications, 1954).

Calwell, A.A., *Labor's Role in Modern Society*, (Melbourne, Lansdowne Press, 1963).

Casey, R.G., *Personal Experience 1939-46* (London, Constable, 1962).

Casey, R.G., *Friends and Neighbours* (Melbourne, F.W. Cheshire. 1954; East Lansing, Michigan State College, 1955).

Crisp, L.F., *Ben Chifley: A Biography* (London, Longmans, Green and Co., 1963).

Mud Map to AUKUS

Dalziel, A., *Evatt the Enigma* (Melbourne, Lansdowne Press, 1967)

Eggleston, F.W., *Reflections on Australian Foreign Policy* (Melbourne, F.W. Cheshire, 1957).

Esthus, Raymond, *From Enmity to Alliance: U.S.-Australian Relations, 1931-1941* (Melbourne University Press, 1964).

Grattan, C.H., *The United States and the Southwest Pacific* (Harvard University Press, 1961).

Greenwood, Gordon, and Harper, N., eds., *Australia in World Affairs 1950-55* (Melbourne, F.W. Cheshire, 1957).

Greenwood, Gordon, and Harper, N., eds., *Australia in World Affairs 1956-60* (Melbourne, F.W. Cheshire, 1963).

Harper, N., and Sissons, D., *Australia and the United Nations* (New York, Manhattan Publishing Co., 1959).

Hasluck, Paul, *The Government and the People – 1939-1941* (Canberra, Australian War Memorial, 1965).

Hudson, W.J., ed., *Towards a Foreign Policy: 1914-1941* (Melbourne, Chassell Australia, 1967).

Levi, W., *American-Australian Relations* (University of Minnesota, 1947).

Mansergh, Nicholas, *Survey of British Commonwealth Affairs: Problems of Wartime Co-operation and Post-war Change 1939-1952*, Royal Institute of

International Affairs, (London, Oxford University Press, 1958).

Matthews, T., "Pressure Groups in Australia ", Mayer, Henry, *Australian Politics: A Reader* (Melbourne, F.W. Cheshire, 1966), pp. 181-220.

Menzies, R.G., *Speech is of Time* (London, Cassell, 1958).

Menzies, R.G., *Afternoon Light: some memories of men and events* (Melbourne, 1967).

Millar, T.B., *Australia's Foreign Policy* (Sydney, Angus and Robertson, 1968).

Modelski, George, ed., *SEATO: Six Studies* (Melbourne, F.W. Cheshire, 1969:).

Rawson, D.W., *Labor in Vain? A Survey of the Australian Labor Party* (Croydon, Longmans, 1966).

Rosecrance, R.N., *Australian Diplomacy and Japan 1945-1951* (Melbourne University Press, 1962).

Schmitt, Bernadette E., "The Relation of Public Opinion and Foreign Affairs Before and During the First World War", Sarkissian, A.O., ed., *Studies in Diplomatic History and Historiography* (London, Longmans, 196), p. 322-330.

Starke, Joseph, *The ANZUS Treaty Alliance* (Melbourne University Press, 1965)

Watt, Alan, *The Evolution of Australian Foreign Policy, 1938-1965* (Cambridge University Press, 1968).

www.ingramcontent.com/pod-product-compliance
Lightning Source LLC
Chambersburg PA
CBHW031142270326
41931CB00007B/669